PENGUIN

YOUNG TAGORE

Sudhir Kakar is a distinguished psychoanalyst and writer. He has written seventeen highly acclaimed books of non-fiction which include, among others, *The Inner World* (now in its sixteenth printing since its first publication in 1978), *Shamans, Mystics and Doctors, Intimate Relations, The Analyst and the Mystic, The Colors of Violence* and *The Indians: Portrait of a People* (with K. Kakar). He has written four novels and his books have been translated into twenty-one languages around the world.

Kakar has taught at leading institutions around the world and has won numerous accolades for his work. Most recently, in February 2012, he was conferred the Order of Merit of the Federal Republic of Germany, the country's highest civilian honour.

PRAISE FOR THE BOOK

'Not only illuminates many nooks and crannies of Tagore's creativity but is in itself an imaginative and luminous meditation on art and life, the body and the soul, and the East and the West'—*Indian Express*

'Refreshing . . . A set of meditations by a thoughtful reader on what Tagore means to him . . . The psychobiographical site where the deepest sources of imagination, joy and suffering can be located. For any psychoanalyst, this is a gift'—*Outlook*

'Paints a fascinating portrait of Tagore seen through the prism of psychological analysis of his own "memory pictures"'—*Sunday Indian*

'Unravels the puzzle that was Tagore . . . A pleasure to read'—*India Today*

SUDHIR KAKAR

YOUNG TAGORE

The Makings of a Genius

PENGUIN BOOKS

An imprint of Penguin Random House

PENGUIN BOOKS

USA | Canada | UK | Ireland | Australia
New Zealand | India | South Africa | China

Penguin Books is part of the Penguin Random House group of companies
whose addresses can be found at global.penguinrandomhouse.com

Published by Penguin Random House India Pvt. Ltd
No: 04-010 to 04-012, 4th Floor, Capital Tower -1,
M G Road, Gurugram -122002, Haryana, India

First published in Viking by Penguin Books India 2013
Published in Penguin Books 2014

Copyright © Sudhir Kakar 2013

Paintings and photographs © Rabindra Bhavana. Reproduced with the
permission of Rabindra Bhavana, Visva-Bharati

Painting on p. 186 © NGMA, New Delhi

10 9 8 7 6 5 4 3 2

ISBN 9780143423386

Typeset in Dante MT by R. Ajith

www.penguin.co.in

For Yana and Rahul

Contents

Preface

Poet, novelist, playwright, composer of songs, painter, philosopher, educationist, Rabindranath Tagore is widely regarded as an outstanding figure in Indian cultural history and the greatest multi-faceted genius India has produced in the last two hundred years. He is also a central figure in India's creative responses to its encounter with the West, responses that have neither retreated into a sullen traditionalism nor uncritically embraced a rootless cosmopolitanism, but have sought to create an idiom that is modern yet at the same time distinctively Indian.

The range of Tagore's creativity is truly astonishing and his oeuvre has been critical to the development of different art forms; besides his literary contributions, Tagore is also widely regarded as the 'father' of modernism in Indian painting, which placed subjectivity at the centre of artistic expression. His significance extends beyond the realm of arts and literature in the sense that he is also an important milestone in the desirable emergence of a modern Indian identity, an Indianness that successfully merges our cultural patrimony with contemporary concerns. As such, he has attracted ample biographical attention, not least in the last couple of years when his 150th birth centenary was celebrated. In Bengali, Prashanta K. Paul's *Rabijibani* (5 vols) and Prabhat Mukhopadhyay's *Rabindra Jibani* (2 vols), in English, Krishna Dutta and Andrew

Robinson's *Rabindranath Tagore: The Myriad-minded Man*, Krishna Kriplani's *Rabindranath Tagore: A Biography* and the more recent Uma Das Gupta's *Rabindranath Tagore: A Biography* and Sabyasachi Bhattacharya's *Rabindranath Tagore: An Interpretation* are a few of the many excellent works which have documented the course of Tagore's life and analysed his work and its place in India's and the world's literary and cultural history.

This slim volume takes a different tack altogether. Focusing on the formative period of Tagore's childhood and youth, it seeks to uncover vital themes in Rabindranath's inner world that had their origins in his early relationships within the family and, together with his spiritual concerns, were later elaborated in the mature artist's sensibility and creative expressions.

In engaging with the life of a 'genius', it is inevitable that one also addresses a question that has fascinated human beings through the centuries: the riddle of extraordinary creativity, which is of a qualitatively different order than the kinds with which we are normally familiar.[1] Whereas ordinary creativity gives us some pleasure and perhaps even an occasional insight, the creative oeuvre of a genius extends the boundaries of his discipline, whether in arts or sciences, and will have a profound influence on its future direction. In attempting to draw a psychological portrait of a creative genius, this book also engages with the biographical perspective on extraordinary creativity.

1

Introduction: Writing the Biography of Inner Life

In his first autobiography, which he began writing around the age
of forty-seven (he was to write another one, shortly before his
death at the age of eighty), Rabindranath Tagore was at pains to
insist in its preamble that it was *not* an autobiography. *Jibansmriti*,
translated into English as *My Reminiscences*, is a collection of 'memory
pictures', he says, not the story of his life. Its writer is not a historian
but 'an unseen artist within', painting original creations on the canvas
of Tagore's memory. Whereas the historian would but record the
external events of life, the artist subtly alters their details and scatters
them with diverse colours that are, in Rabindranath's words, 'passion-
tinged from his heart'.[1]

In his selection of emotionally compelling memories and
garbing them in literary grace, Tagore is one of a small number
of autobiographers whose recollections are highly individual and
yet possess a wider, universal appeal. Like the Irish poet W.B. Yeats,
who found *Jibansmriti* a 'rich and most valuable work', Tagore,
too, has the power of giving voice to general truths that underlie
intense personal experiences. Consciously or unconsciously, the
poet Tagore is spurred by his aesthetic Muse into transforming the
narration of his memories into literature. As distinct from most

autobiographies of men and women who have achieved eminence in public or intellectual life, the aesthetic distance created by a literary reworking of memories, both expressing and cushioning the impact of agonizing emotions, promises the reader insights into troubling episodes of his own life, thus allowing and even encouraging him to reconnect with their painful emotions and integrate them into his life history.

I view the opening sentences of *Jibansmriti* as an invitation to a psychological biographer to mine them for emotional truths rather than facts and thus lay bare the deeper motivations of Rabindranath's life and work that are not available (or even possible) in his 'historical' biographies. I do not mean to imply that the distinction between historical and psychological biography is unbridgeable. It is not as if a psychological biographer neglects the outer events of his subject's life. Not aiming for a comprehensive account of a life from birth to death, what a psychological biography does is to be selective of the 'events' on which it concentrates. Essentially, the psychological biographer believes that the events which comprise his subject's formative experiences lie in the periods of his childhood and early youth and that a person's 'psychological truth' is pre-eminently an outcome of his or her early relationships.

On the other hand, historical biographers, in setting out the events of a person's life, making connections and drawing conclusions, also make psychological observations and attribute motivations to the subject's actions, if only to give their work a narrative power that makes a biography readable. Indeed, the finest practitioners of the craft, either through a long immersion in the life and writings of the subject or gifted with the psychological intuition of an outstanding novelist, have produced compelling psychological portraits.[2]

In general, though, without clinical experience and unfamiliar with the nuances of depth psychology and thus untrained to look for the kind of information pertaining to the hidden areas of a subject's life, historical biographers often struggle in presenting a convincing psychological portrait of their subjects. The subject of a historical biography may come through as 'great' in achievement, yet remain distant as a person of flesh and blood, devoid of an inner life we are all familiar with through our own subjectivity.

The inner biography I am attempting here is not to be confused with 'psychoanalysis of Tagore' although, I fear, my protestation will be of little avail in escaping this pejorative appellation. In a clinical psychoanalysis, the analyst and the analysand jointly construct the latter's inner story as much through the analysand's talking as through the analyst 'listening with the third ear' to the intonations, lapses and the silences in the flow of his speech. The latter dimension is inevitably lacking in the written materials available to one who would be a biographer of an inner life. Autobiographical writings, diaries and letters can never have the spontaneity of speech in the clinical setting since they are invariably edited to varying degrees in the process of being penned on paper or, increasingly, typed in on the computer screen. The kind of information in the clinical situation that leads to the construction of a psychoanalytic biography of the patient—his or her musings on people and events of daily life, full-blown fantasies and dreams, including the memorable and highly impactful 'big dreams', and the associations to which they give rise, memories of earlier periods of life and their revisiting and reworking over the course of analysis—is never available to the same degree of richness to someone who would write a psychological biography of a historical figure.

In drawing a rough map of the subject's inner terrain, capturing its essential features though missing the telling details that only gradually emerge during the course of an analysis, the ambitions of the psychobiographer are necessarily limited. What I would like to do here is unfold the plot of Rabindranath's inner life in a manner that has the narrative qualities of consistency, coherence and intelligibility, while recognizing that in absence of the kind of data that is available in the clinical situation, a psychological biography will be more speculative—also in the original meaning of the term, speculari, descrying something that is hidden.[3] I would even argue that the quality of a psychobiography is intimately related to the sophistication of its speculation. As imaginative reconstruction, speculation can spy out hidden truths and deserves a place of honour even in historical biography which emphasizes a prudent adjudication of facts as its ideal.

On the other hand, in contrast to the analyst who encounters the patient for a period of time at a certain stage of his life, the psychobiographer has an overview of a whole life, of knowing 'how it all turned out'. His task is also made easier with creative artists like Rabindranath who have poured their inner life into their work. The psychobiographer may also have a slight advantage over the analyst in that his information on the subject, though of a lesser order, is not limited to the subject himself but also comes from other sources—family members, friends, contemporaries—unavailable in the privacy of the consulting room. This information on the 'social self' of the subject must not be dismissed lightly, since a consistent finding of psychological research is that people are fairly accurate in their perceptions of others but have distorted perceptions of themselves.

There are, however, elements of clinical psychoanalysis that I believe the writer of an inner biography shares with the analyst, elements that can be subsumed under the rubric of 'psychoanalytic sensibility'. Since there has been no single approach to the writing of an inner biography and psychobiographers have emphasized different aspects of psychoanalytic sensibility,[4] I will list elements of this sensibility which have guided my own exploration of Rabindranath's inner life.

For me, the biographer's *empathy*, an openness to and participation in the emotions of his subject's writings, a reading, so to speak,

with the third eye as a counterpoint to the analyst's listening with
the third ear, is the very foundation of a psychological biography.
Empathy, a 'feeling into' the subject through the medium of his
writings, a partaking of his inner experiences through an unconscious
attunement, is a demanding task. It requires that our normal non-
empathetic state, a state of self-experience with thoughts that are
usually self-related, change into a state where we can transcend the
boundaries of the self to share the conscious and unconscious feelings
and experiences of another self. My starting point, then, is to pay
careful attention to the resonances in my own psyche as I read Tagore's
autobiographical and other writings. Only after an exploration of my
own emotional reactions to Tagore's description of an 'event' in his
life may I go into the elucidatory mode, using additional biographical
and other information, as also psychoanalytic findings, for a more
conscious understanding of the meaning of that particular event.
My approach is then similar to the Germanist Emil Staiger's credo
of poetics: '*Zu begreifen was uns ergreift*'—to grasp what has gripped
us, or in other words, apprehending precedes comprehension, where
it is important that the latter is not wedded to any rigid theoretical
framework. Emotional participation in the autobiographical narration
of the formative experiences of Tagore's life and their reflection in
his stories, poems and paintings are thus combined with a flexibility
in the use of psychoanalytical theories in striving to understand the
meaning of the key scenes of his inner theatre.

Empathy, of course, is not something that can be consciously
willed but arises from contemplation rather than effortful striving
and will always be plagued by the doubt whether its highly subjective,
experiential character is not merely a projection of the biographer's
own feelings, fantasies and wishes on to the subject. Freud, who
doubted that biographical truth was ever possible,[5] yet himself
wrote biographical sketches of the inner life of historical figures
anyway (Leonardo da Vinci, Woodrow Wilson), was quite aware

of the temptation of an unconscious transference of feelings from the biographer's past projected on to the subject of the biography, a temptation that *all* biographers, historical or psychological, face when they embark on the project of writing a life. He writes:

> In many cases (biographers) have chosen their hero as the subject of their studies because—for reasons of their own emotional life—they have felt a special affection for him from the very first. They then devote their energies to a task of idealization, aimed at enrolling the great man among the class of their infantile models—at reviving in him perhaps, the child's idea of his father . . . they thus present us with what is in fact a cold, strange, ideal figure, instead of a human being to whom we might feel ourselves distantly related. That they should do this is regrettable, for they thereby sacrifice truth to illusion, and for the sake of their infantile phantasies abandon the opportunity of penetrating the most fascinating secrets of human nature.[6]

Empathy, then, also calls for an introspective exploration of the biographer's own emotional stance towards his subject, both pre-existing and the changes it undergoes as he engages more deeply with the subject, including the less than conscious transferences to him from significant figures in the biographer's own early life.

Here, I will give only a sketchy account of the obstacles to and the course of my own empathy as I began to involve myself in Tagore's life and writings.

Growing up and well into adulthood, I was never attracted to Tagore. Like any middle-class Indian boy, I was aware of his literary stature, and had even read one of his stories, 'The Kabuliwala', in a school textbook but had always felt vaguely repelled by his flamboyant appearance in photographs where he always seemed to be clad in a loose robe that came down to the ankles, wore shoulder-length long hair and sported a flowing beard that framed a grave, unsmiling face. He reminded me of Bhagwan Rajneesh (or Osho as he was known later), though without the latter's endearing mischievousness. I had skimmed through Tagore's own translation of the poems of *Gitanjali* , his Nobel Prize-winning work, and with the callowness of youth dismissed them as verses of stereotyped sentimentality and saccharine spirituality. Without giving it much thought, I was ready to give credence to the rumour that no one in the Nobel committee for literature had heard of him or read his work before W.B. Yeats recommended *Gitanjali* for the prize in 1914 and that, given the politics of the prize, it was time for an Asian laureate. I was thus in no danger of idealizing Tagore; the pitfall lay more in my minimizing of his stature, in his devaluation.

Not that I was not intrigued by the veneration in which my Bengali friends held him. The bulk of Indian writings on Tagore and his work came from Bengal, as they continue to do so till this day. I found this shared fascination, which seemed to be an unwritten commandment that a Bengali intellectual or creative artist, including some of the most eminent ones—Amartya Sen, Satyajit Ray, Amitav Ghosh, Amit Chaudhuri, Ashis Nandy, Sunil Gangopadhyay come immediately to mind—must engage with Gurudev (as he was reverently addressed in his old age) at some point of his life, an endearing mystery of the Bengali character. In social gatherings it was *de rigueur* for my Bengali friends, men and women, to join in the communal singing of his songs, the Rabindrasangeet (which I found quite monotonous and listened to it with an expression of polite, though baffled, interest), with the rapturous expressions of devotees in a bhajan assembly. I realize, of course, that whereas I was only reacting to the aesthetics of the music with my uninitiated ears, they were reliving all the associations connected with the songs they had heard and sung since childhood: the less than conscious memories of family occasions where the joint singing had erased any discordant notes in family life, the social gatherings in youth and adulthood where the songs had removed barriers of distance, reinforced bonds of friendship and made them feel part of a larger community. I believe that the identity-giving power of Rabindrasangeet, buttressing a social, Bengali identity that can counteract personal disquiets, even if temporarily, does not have a counterpart in any of India's other linguistic groups.

My shallow stance towards Tagore, which I now recollect with some shame, was fuelled by an early identification with my father's attitudes. He, as I have recounted elsewhere, was a man of no-nonsense rationality, deeply suspicious of India's mystics and gurus. Even as an aficionado of Sanskrit poetry, my father preferred the scepticism of a Bhartrihari to a 'romantic' Kalidasa.[7] Of the English writers, he admired people like Bernard Shaw and Bertrand Russell, both of whom were condescendingly dismissive of Tagore. Tagore was also the recipient of my more hidden, negative feelings towards my father in that I believed that Gurudev had been a foe of Indian nationalism represented by Gandhi, someone who received his knighthood from the British (which he later returned) only because he had served the Raj well, as had my father.

Then, two years ago, I was invited by the National Gallery of Modern Art in New Delhi to give a talk on Tagore's paintings as part of his 150th birthday celebrations. I accepted, challenged as much by the opportunity to discover Tagore as by the novel task of engaging with a visual medium rather than my normal province of language and words. The discovery was momentous. Tagore's 'spirituality', which I had once airily dismissed as naïve nature mysticism, revealed itself as a profound feeling of kinship, an empathetic connection, with the earth and the plants, trees, birds, animals and, indeed, all life forms that it sustains. The solemn, lushly bearded visage of the rishi of my childhood mythology peering out from his photographs, which I had once instinctively distrusted, now revealed itself as a mask protecting the vulnerability of a highly sensitive man, a profound introvert who must have suffered in a world that often demanded he be an extravert. There is nothing quite as stressful as an introvert forced to be an extravert. And as I engaged with his life and became engrossed in his writings, I came to like RT (my private name for him) more and more. A liking of the subject, the prerequisite for empathy, as long as it limits itself to admiration, is a must for an intending biographer of inner life. This is where the psychological biographer essentially differs from his historical counterpart for whom liking and dislike of the subject are largely irrelevant. Indeed, there are 'many instances of great historians who have been at daggers drawn with their subjects',[8] a stance that is impossible for a psychological biographer.[9]

The pitfalls awaiting the psychobiographer are of a different order. The danger I faced as I immersed myself in Rabindranath's life and writings was of my mounting admiration ascending into an idealization that is a feature of much of the scholarship on Tagore, especially among some Bengali scholars who are so possessive of him that they dismiss any attempts by an outsider to fathom the mystery of his genius. Given his polymathic and philosophical breadth, his torrential output that reminds one of Rilke's words about Rodin, 'It's like holding a cup beneath a waterfall', I had to be careful that the pendulum did not swing the other way, from an initial mild distaste to an outright idealization that can make one tentative and shy away from pursuing insights that reveal the face under the public mask.

The second element of psychoanalytic sensibility is attending to the *key themes* that get repeated again and again during the course of a person's life. These themes, which have their origins and get established in our earliest relationships during infancy and childhood, are then articulated in ways suited to the particular stage of life; a young man loves differently than a child, an old woman weeps differently than a girl. A life theme is like the recurring musical motif in a symphony that is taken up by different instruments at different moments in the symphonic unfolding or, in Indian classical music, like the initial *sthayi* in the exposition of a raga which generates many musical ideas but to which the singer will return again and again. The origins and earliest expression of these themes lie veiled in forgetfulness, an inner theatre that took place behind the heavy curtain of our conscious memory but one which we can descry in our dreams and fantasies, wishes and fears, actions and works, through enduring introspection.

To the two elements of psychoanalytic sensibility that I believe are essential in undertaking an inner biography—empathy that uses one's own psyche as an instrument, and attention to key psychological themes in the subject's life—one must also add that the psychobiographer needs some understanding of the zeitgeist of the era, the 'spirit of the times', in which his subject lived. In Rabindranath's case, the zeitgeist is that of Bengal in the second half of the nineteenth century under British rule, mediated to the child, Rabi, by his upper-class Brahmin family that was unorthodox in many ways as it sought to negotiate the divide between its Hindu tradition and a West-inspired modernity. To adapt an observation by the child psychologist Rene Spitz, the baby Rabi was born without a history; very soon his parents and the Tagore family of Jorasanko in Calcutta would give him theirs. I imagine that Tagore would not disagree—'The sculptor who created me began his handiwork with Bengali clay. The rough contours of an initial likeness took shape. That was my childhood, made of pure stuff with few admixtures. Most of the ingredients were stored up within my own self, while some other elements were determined by the atmosphere and people at home.'[10] I would only add that both the 'pure stuff' and the stored up 'ingredients' were substantially products of Rabi's experiences in his early relationships within the family, beginning with his mother, Sharada Devi.

2

The Paradise

For someone whose memory pictures of his past are filled with telling detail and brushed in with glowing colours, someone who compares himself to 'the road in the night listening to the footfalls of its memories in silence',[1] Tagore's one memory of his mother in his *Reminiscences*—her death and the effect it had on him—leaves one bewildered. The chapter 'Bereavements', almost at the end of that book, begins with these passages:

> In the meantime, death made its appearance in our family. Before this I had never met Death face to face. When my mother died I was quite a child. She had been ailing for quite a long time, and we did not even know when her malady took a fatal turn. She used all along to sleep on a separate bed in the same room with us. Then in the course of her illness she was taken for a boat trip on the river, and on her return a room on the third storey of the inner apartments was set apart for her.
>
> On the night she died we were fast asleep in our room downstairs. At what hour I cannot tell, our old nurse came running in weeping and crying: 'O my little ones, you have lost your all!' My sister-in-law rebuked her and led her away, to save us the

15

sudden shock of death at night. Half awakened by her words, I felt my heart sink within me but could not make out what had happened. When in the morning we were told of her death, I could not realize all that it meant for me as we came out into the verandah and saw my mother laid on a bedstead in the courtyard. There was nothing in her appearance which showed death to be terrible. The aspect which death wore in that morning light was as lovely as a calm and peaceful sleep, and the gulf between life and its absence was not brought home to us.

Only when her body was taken out by the main gateway, and we followed the procession to the cremation ground, did a storm of grief pass through me at the thought that Mother would never return by this door and again take her accustomed place in the affairs of the household. The day wore on, we returned from the cremation, and as we turned into our lane I looked up towards my father's rooms on the third storey. He was still sitting in the front verandah, motionless in prayer.

She who was the youngest daughter-in-law took charge of the motherless little ones. She herself saw to our food and clothing and all our other wants, and kept us constantly near, so that we might not feel our loss too keenly. One of the characteristics of the living is the power to heal the irreplaceable, to forget the irreplaceable. And in early life this power is strongest, so that no blow penetrates too deeply, no scar is left permanently. Thus the first shadow of death which fell upon us left no darkness behind; it departed as softly as it came, only as a shadow.[2]

This memory, however, does not relate to a child of six or seven, as a casual reader may conclude. Rabindranath was fourteen when his mother died, not the small child of his memory who was not fully aware of the mother's illness. I am also intrigued by his talk of 'motherless little ones' and the youngest daughter-in-law who 'kept us constantly near, so that we might not feel our loss too keenly'. The fourteen-year-old Rabindranath, the fourteenth living child of his parents, was the youngest in the family at the time of Sharada Devi's death. All his other siblings, except one, were already adult men and women, most with families of their own. Some of these families, of the brothers, lived together in the ancestral house. It is also surprising to read, from someone who possessed an extraordinary empathy for children and has written some of the most insightful poetry and stories about what goes on in a child's soul, that in early life, 'no blow penetrates too deeply, no scar is permanent', when we know that the truth is its opposite, that a child is especially vulnerable because of its relative lack of protective defences, the bulwark around a delicate soul.

Memory, we know, is a cloth whose weave of past events is woven with the weft of fears, wishes and conflicts of the one who is now remembering. The English poet William Wordsworth, alludes to this double nature of memory, 'I cannot say what portion is in truth / The naked recollection of that time / And what may rather have been call'd to life / By after-meditation.'[3] He compares memory with a view of water from a moving boat where the traveller is confused by the 'many things reflected / and at the bottom of the deep / . . . often is perplex'd, and cannot part / The shadow from the substance.'[4] Little wonder that although in ancient Greece, Mnemosyne, the goddess of memory, was honoured as the mother of the Muses, she also had the reputation of being a liar.

Rabindranath, I feel, is trying to express something about the meaning of his mother's death that another part of him is trying to conceal. What I sense here is the reflection of a struggle taking place below the surface of awareness between the facing of an emotional truth and its denial. The memory, with all its scenes, including the one with the father on the third storey 'still sitting in the front verandah, motionless in prayer' (Did he not go to his wife's cremation? Is 'motionless' an expression of absorption in grief, or indifference?) is symbolic of a whole aspect of the poet's early childhood. I feel its discrepancies and incongruities, a sensing by the reader of sentiments unvoiced and thoughts left unsaid, are because of the distortions that took place in the memory picture in the act of his painting it. Such distortions are not only due to memory's acts of omission and commission but also because of the interference of powerful emotions that have, so to speak, yet to be metabolized.

To look for a possible reason for the distortions in his autobiographical memory, it is important to know when and why Tagore wrote *Jibansmriti*.[5] Although published in 1911, Tagore says that he began exploring the 'picture-chamber' some years earlier. The autobiography was thus begun at a time following a string of personal losses: his wife died in 1902, his twelve-year-old daughter Renuka in 1903, his father in 1905 and in 1907, perhaps the most grievous loss, the death of his youngest and favourite son, the eleven-year-old Samindranath, from cholera. In the absence of other motives that are often advanced by persons engaged in the 'strange task' of recounting the story of their lives for an audience—adding to the historical record or refurbishing one's reputation, as in the case of most people in public life, the wish to persuade or convert (St Augustine), to instruct how to live a good life in harmony with one's era (Goethe), to help others, especially the youth to live a moral life (Gandhi)—I would surmise that for Tagore the writing of *Jibansmriti* was pre-eminently an attempt at restoring an emptying self, depleted by losses of the preceding years. An excursion into childhood and youth often evokes soothing effects. This is so even when one is recollecting their painful episodes, if they have been integrated in the story of one's life, when the original pain is now but a slight twinge and is generally passed over with a rueful smile. It is only when memory comes across a cut-off part of the self that has not yet been consciously integrated and demands a peremptory hearing that seeks such an integration, that the autobiographical writing is apt to stumble.

Before I attempt to explore the cut-off part of the self in Rabi's relationship and experience with his mother, I would like to get some sense of her as a person—a difficult task, considering the paucity of material that exists on Sharada Devi, and the gulfs of culture and time (and gender) that separate us.

The picture one gets from the scattered remarks of her family is of a conventional Hindu wife of nineteenth century Bengal, devoted to her husband and children.[6] She was deeply religious, undertaking all the rituals for the welfare and longevity of her husband which have been prescribed by Hindu scriptures, and by the dictates of the Brahmo faith of the family she had married into.

Since the Tagore family was wealthy, Sharada Devi had a good deal of leisure. As in most aristocratic families, she spent her days and nights in the women's quarters, where she would recline on a divan while the maids applied beauty preparations known as *rooptan* to her daughters-in-law and Sharada Devi listened to the complaints of the women of the *andar mahal* and mediated their quarrels.[7] In Jorasanko, as in all aristocratic Bengali houses, the living quarters of men, women and older children were separated from each other, their lives poles apart. No man, unless a close relative, ever entered the women's quarters. On her rare trips outside home, like other women in the Tagore household, Sharada Devi always went in a covered palanquin, the palki. The outings were limited to visiting relatives on important social occasions such as a wedding when the palki would be carried right into the inner courtyard of the women's quarters. For a bath in the holy Ganges, the bearers would dip the palki in the river, with the women inside.[8] If a woman ever came face to face with a man not from her own family, she would instantly draw down the pallu of her sari to veil her face and turn her back to the man.

What lends a touch of colour to Sharada Devi's otherwise pallid portrait is the fact that she became literate after marriage and was very fond of reading popular texts like *Shishu-bodhak*, a mix of folktales, proverbs, edifying maxims, as also the epics Ramayana and Mahabharata. She often asked her sons to read the Sanskrit version of the epics, delighting in the sound of the language even if she was unable to understand it. She did not share the popular belief, more prevalent in rural Bengal, that literacy in a woman would lead to her becoming a widow.

Although absent in his *Reminiscences*, we are offered Rabindranath's own portrait of his mother in his second autobiography, *My Boyhood Days*, written for the children of his school in Shantiniketan shortly before his death. The picture is still sketchy but one senses that the cut-off part of the self in relation to his mother is now better accommodated. There is vivid detail and gentle wit in the few scenes that feature Sharada Devi, a sign that the emotional conflict that caused a disturbance of memory in the earlier autobiography has been largely resolved and a major reconciliation with the past has taken place. It is my general impression that in the autobiographical recollections of his old age, although they recount many of the same events, Tagore is generally more dispassionate than in his earlier *Reminiscences* where the feelings— anxiety, despair, bliss— associated with memories of his emotional experiences, are relatively more prominent.

Scene 1. Indulgent mother collaborating with the boy's wish to miss a lesson by pretending to be sick.

...I never felt the symptoms of indigestion that manifest themselves in stomach ache, though I would complain of the condition to my mother. Ma would listen to me in secret amusement, without appearing worried in the least. All the same, she would summon the attendant and instruct him, 'Very well, go and tell the tutor that he can take the day off.'[9]

Scene 2. In mock exasperation, much like Yashoda's in relation to the child Krishna, mother subordinating her own needs to that of the son.

When it grew dark. . .I would head for my mother's room. Ma would then be playing cards with her khuri, or paternal aunt. The room with its patterned parquet floor gleamed like ivory, the enormous bedstead covered with an embroidered, quilted spread. I would make such a nuisance of myself that she would fling down her hand of cards and exclaim, 'What a troublesome boy! Go, Khuri, tell him a story.'[10]

Scene 3. Admiring mother, bedazzled by her brilliant son.

I remember the walled terrace of the interior portion of our house. In the evening, Ma would spread a floor-mat of woven reed, and chat with the female companions who surrounded her. . .Before this circle I would sometime display my learning, freshly gleaned from textbooks. The sun was ten million miles away from the earth, I would tell them. From *Rijupath Part 2*, I recited a chunk of *Valmiki Ramayana*, no less, Sanskrit diction and all. Ma had no way of gauging her son's accuracy of pronunciation, but the brilliance of his learning extended along the sun's ten-million-mile-long trajectory to dazzle her, all the same. Who would have thought that such shlokas could be recited by anyone other than sage Narada?[11]

These memories are from later childhood when Rabi was no longer living with his mother and other women of the family in the *andar mahal* but had a room outside in the children's quarters of the sprawling Tagore mansion. In the absence of recollections before the age of six, how do we access the memories of Rabi's earliest childhood? How can we get even an inkling of the flitting shadows in the primordial cave at the dawn of consciousness and their more stable representations as his consciousness took a tenuous hold?

If there is one uncontested finding in the writings of psychoanalysts, of whatever persuasion, over the last hundred years, then it is the defining role of the first caretaker, usually the mother, in the development of a person's inner life. The bond with her constitutes the first and most important building block in the structure of the human psyche, forming a person's basic pattern of being in the world, comprising the notes of his life's signature tune. Recent research in psychology and neurosciences have confirmed the vital role of the first relationship. In an infant's brain that is creating 1.8 million neural connections per second, the relationship with the mother and the love flowing through this connection which wires the baby's brain, is crucial. Indeed, the importance of this connection extends to other species as well; the more a rat pup is licked and groomed by its mother, the more synaptic connections it has.

If Tagore's declarative memory, the system that provides the basis for conscious recollection of facts and events, is not available for all that took place in Rabi's bond with his mother in infancy and early childhood, must a biographer of his inner life admit defeat? By no means if one agrees with Nietzsche that every great philosophy is a species of involuntary and unconscious autobiography. In the case of some scholars and scientists, he adds, 'there may really be such a thing as an "impulse to knowledge", some kind of small, independent clockwork, which, when well wound up, works away industriously to that end'.[12] I would go further and add that the work of not only the philosopher but also of the artist, the writer, and of many a creative scholar in the humanities is inspired by the fundamental impulses of their nature that are embedded in and have been shaped

by the course of their lives. I believe that original work takes place
only when the areas of enquiry carved out by the individual as his
own resonate with the major themes of his life that are played out
below the surface of his conscious awareness. Insights dawn, and
are more often one's lot, when the work is but a preconscious or an
unconscious continuation of one's inner theatre, of one's biography
in another register.

Along with other psychoanalytic writers, I believe that the works
of a creative writer or painter can afford us access to memories
that are not consciously available to him,[13] a view also endorsed by
Goethe who maintained that a lyric poem reveals its author. In other
words, Tagore's poems, stories and plays (and paintings) are in part
emotional autobiographies even if we may not be able to decipher
the play and complexity of his emotional reactions, including those
related to his mother, in but a rudimentary fashion. I believe Tagore
would agree. Writing about his second collection of poems, he says
that they are the story of a struggle between his inner and outer
selves that he tried to resolve in the poetry. He goes on to observe,
'As in all creation, so in poetry there is an opposition of forces. If the
divergence is too wide, or the unison too close, there is, it seems to
me, no room for poetry. Where the pain of discord strives to attain
and express its resolution into harmony, then does poetry break forth
into music, as breath through a flute.'[14]

In other words, a poem is a reworking of an inner conflict that
is made possible by the aesthetic distance promised, and demanded,
by poetry. In a later chapter, I will come back to the source of the
'aesthetic distance' and what made it possible.

In the above quote, Tagore is referring to his poems in *Evening
Songs* but his observations apply equally to the poems of *The Crescent
Moon*, which contain a large number of poems on mother and child.[15]
What Rabindranath could not say in *Jibansmriti*, he could express in
these poems; the two belong together.

Sharada Devi was forty-four years old when Rabi was born, an age at which most Bengali (and Indian) women were grandmothers, as was Sharada. Elsewhere, I have discussed the identity-giving power of a son's birth for the traditional Indian woman.[16] This identity is organized around the core of 'motherliness', with its central expressions of tenderness, nurturing and protectiveness towards the infant—a motherliness which is the core element for the traditional woman's identity in a way that it may not be for the more modern woman today. And in nineteenth century Bengal, in absence of other models, motherliness was the sole identity option that was available to women, even to most women in the Tagore family, which was advanced for its times. The high emotional investment in the son, demanded by the centrality of motherliness in her identity as a woman, must have been markedly enhanced in Sharada Devi's case by the fact that Rabi was a fruit of old loins who—after the death of another child, Budhendra, in early infancy—would remain the 'baby' of the family and thus a special object of the mother's affection and care.

Let us then look at Rabi's experience of his mother's emotional engagement with the infant in the poems of *The Crescent Moon*. Although these poems were written to divert his young children after the death of their mother, Rabindranath makes it abundantly clear in his letters that his intention in these poems was also to recreate his own early childhood. [17]As I have said earlier, 'looking' for me means both a feeling into the poem and understanding it in the sense of deciphering an unconscious purpose behind the conscious intention. The poet Rabindranath would only concur with the first part of the enterprise: 'So when after listening to a poem anyone says he has not understood it, I feel nonplussed. If someone smells a flower and says he does not understand, the reply to him is: 'There is nothing to understand, it is only a scent. . .Like a tear or a smile, it is but a picture of what is taking place within. If Science or Philosophy may gain anything from it they are welcome, but that is not the reason of its being.' [18]

Reflecting upon his own experiences as a twelve-year-old hearing the sonorous Sanskrit of the gayatri mantra or reading Jayadeva's *Gita Govinda*—both without understanding the meaning of the words but (like his mother) thrilling to their sounds and the lilt of the metre in Jayadeva's poetry that filled his mind with pictures of grace—Rabindranath is convinced that to be clear about the meaning of words is not the most important part of the process of human understanding and that whoever 'goes back to his childhood will agree that his greatest gains were not in proportion to the completeness of his understanding'.[19] But, unlike the poet and begging his indulgence, the prose writer, however much he may appreciate the scent of the rose, remains a botanist, not a gardener. Understanding and feeling into a poem or a work of art are not contradictory as some poets and artists would have it. Although I too would reject the notion that meaning is a construction, that 'Truth lies in the interpretation', I am equally hesitant to embrace its opposite, 'Truth, *lies* in the interpretation.'

Evoked by his mother's voice, it is from 'some primal world of infancy lost in twilit consciousness',[20] from which these poems arise. Some of them reflect an internal bond that belongs to neither alone, a fusion in which their selves feel so permeable to each other that it doesn't matter whose body is whose, where the mother wishes '. . .I could take a quiet corner in the heart of my baby's very own world' and 'travel by the road that crosses my baby's mind. . .'[21] or, in another, 'When I kiss your face to make you smile, my darling, I surely understand what pleasure streams from the sky in the morning light, and what delight the summer breeze brings to my body—when I kiss to make you smile.'[22]

In others, the infant son is the physical manifestation of the mother's deepest desires and her feminine essence.

'Where have I come from, where did you pick me up?' the baby asked its mother.
She answered half crying, half laughing, and clasping the baby to her breast—
'You were hidden in my heart as its desire, my darling.
. . .
When in girlhood my heart was opening its petals, you hovered as a fragrance about it.
Your tender softness bloomed in my youthful limbs, like a glow in the sky before sunrise.'[23]

There are 'memories' of a playful absorption in each other—'I will be waves and you will be a strange shore/ I shall roll on and on, and break upon your lap with laughter'[24]—and the hide and seek games of the toddler, attended with the fear of actually getting lost, transformed into lyrical poetry.

Supposing I became a champa flower, just for fun, and grew on a branch high up that tree, and shook in the wind with laughter and danced upon the newly budded leaves, would you know me, mother?
You would call, 'Baby, where are you?' and I should laugh to myself and keep quite quiet.
I should slyly open my petals and watch you at your work.
When after your bath, with wet hair spread on your shoulders, you walked through the shadow of the champa tree to the little court where you say your prayers, you would notice the scent of the flower, but not know that it came from me.
. . .
When in the evening you went to the cow-shed with the lighted lamp in your hand, I should suddenly drop on the earth again and be your own baby once more, and beg you to tell me a story.

'Where have you been, you naughty child?'
'I won't tell you, mother.'
That's what I would say then.[25]

There are unconscious memories of Krishna-like sulks, so beloved in
Indian dance forms and in the bhajans, thumris and dadras of light
classical music. There are also memories of other minor disquiets as
the infant becomes a toddler and begins to explore the world while
still tied to the mother with an emotional string, disquiets that end in
reinforcing rather than weakening their bond as 'his little cries over
tiny troubles weave the double bond of pity and love'.[26]

> If I were only a little puppy, not your baby, mother dear, would
> you say 'No' to me if I tried to eat from your dish?
> Would you drive me off, saying to me, 'get away, you naughty
> little puppy?'
> Then go, mother, go! I will never come to you when you call me,
> and never let you feed me any more.[27]

And then there are poems of little Rabi at what psychoanalysts would
call the 'eve of Oedipus', when the three- to four-year-old child's
love affair with the mother and the maternal universe is at its height
before it is impinged upon by the world of men represented, above
all, by the father. The poems of this stage have the boy fantasizing
about himself as an adventurer who ranges far and wide but always
returns to the mother to bask in her admiration of his exploits.

> We shall set sail in early morning light.
> When at noontide you are bathing at the pond, we shall be in
> the land of a strange king. When we come back it will be getting
> dark, and I shall tell you of all that we have seen. I shall cross the
> seven seas and the thirteen rivers of fairyland.[28]

And also:

> Mother, if you don't mind, I should like to become the boatman
> of the ferryboat when I am grown up.
> I shall cross and cross back from bank to bank, and all the boys
> and girls of the village will wonder at me while they are bathing.
> . . .
> When the day is done and the shadows cower under the trees, I
> shall come back after dusk.
> I shall never go away from you into the town to work like father.
> Mother, if you don't mind, I should like to become the boatman
> of the ferryboat when I am grown up.[29]

In his fantasy of the hero, he is a slayer of demons and the scourge
of villains who would harm his mother, not the little Rabi of reality
who was mortally afraid of ghosts and spirits that lurked among the
trees and bushes of the garden at night and haunted the dimly lit
hallways of the Jorasanko mansion.

> Mother, let us imagine we are traveling, and passing through a
> strange and dangerous country.
> You are riding in a palanquin and I am trotting by you on a red
> horse.
> It is evening and the sun goes down. The waste of *Joradighi* lies
> wan and grey before us. The land is desolate and barren.
> You are frightened and thinking—'I know not where we have
> come to.'
> I say to you, 'Mother, do not be afraid.'
> The meadow is prickly with spiky grass, and through it runs a
> narrow broken path.
> There are no cattle to be seen in the wide field; they have gone
> to their village stalls.

Suddenly you call me and ask me in a whisper, 'What light is that near the bank?'

Just then there bursts out a fearful yell, and figures come running towards us.

You sit crouched in your palanquin and repeat the names of the gods in prayer.

The bearers, shaking in terror, hide themselves in the thorny bush.

I shout to you, 'Don't be afraid, mother. I am here.'

With long sticks in their hands and hair all wild about their heads, they come nearer and nearer.

I shout, 'Have a care! You villains! One step more and you are dead men.'

They give another terrible yell and rush forward.

You clutch my hand and say, 'Dear boy, for heaven's sake, keep away from them.'

I say, 'Mother, just you watch me.'

Then I spur my horse for a wild gallop, and my sword and buckler clash against each other.

The fight becomes so fearful, mother, that it would give you a cold shudder could you see it from your palanquin.

Many of them fly, and a great number are cut to pieces.

I know you are thinking, sitting all by yourself, that your boy must be dead by this time.

But I come to you all stained with blood, and say, 'Mother, the fight is over now.'

You come out and kiss me, pressing me to your heart, and you say to yourself,

'I don't know what I should do if I hadn't my boy to escort me. . .'[30]

A discordant note in the melodious duet of mother and son is introduced as the father now enters the scene. Indeed, the four- to five-year-old Rabi could not have failed to notice the change in his mother whenever Debendranath returned home from his frequent travels. Tagore's elder sister-in-law Jnanadanandini, whom Rabindranath would get close to in his youth, tells us in her recollections, *Puratani*, that Sharada always personally went into the kitchen to supervise the cooking of her husband's meals. She would change into a freshly laundered cotton saree and spray herself with scent when Debendranath called for her in his room late at night.[31] Poems in *The Crescent Moon* tell us about the boy's awareness that he is not the sole focus of his mother's attention, his wish to replace the rival who has intruded into their two-person universe, and the sinking feeling of his looming defeat in an unequal contest.

> Why do you sit there on the floor so quiet and silent, tell me, mother dear?
> The rain is coming in through the open window, making you all wet, and you don't mind it.
> What has happened to you that you look so strange?
> Haven't you got a letter from father today?[32]

. . .

> I am small because I am a little child, I shall be big when I am as old as my father is.
> . . .
> In the holiday time in October father will come home and, thinking that I am still a baby, will bring for me from the town little shoes and small silken frocks.
> I shall say, 'Father, give them to my elder brother, for I am as big as you are.'[33]

But now comes the traumatic blow—Rabi's banishment from the *andar mahal* to the servants' quarters, the exile from a paradise

now irretrievably lost, a separation that is like death itself. In a
poignant poem aptly titled 'The End', Rabindranath transforms
the melancholy that floods into the gaping hole in his heart into
a yearning for a reunion 'felt more deeply and fully' and one that
the child believes is not his longing alone but also that of the
mother.

> It is time for me to go, mother; I am going.
>
> When in the paling darkness of the lonely dawn you stretch
> out your arms for your baby in the bed, I shall say, 'Baby is not
> there!'—mother, I am going.
>
> I shall become a delicate draught of air and caress you; and I
> shall be ripples in the water when you bathe, and kiss you and
> kiss you again.
>
> . . .
>
> On the straying moonbeams I shall steal over your bed, and lie
> upon your bosom while you sleep.
>
> I shall become a dream, and through the little opening of your
> eyelids I shall slip into the depths of your sleep; and when you
> wake up and look startled, like a twinkling firefly I shall flit out
> into the darkness,
>
> When, on the great festival of puja, the neighbor's children come
> and play about the house, I shall melt into the music of the flute
> and throb in your heart all day.
>
> Dear auntie will come with puja-presents and will ask, 'Where is
> our baby, sister? Mother, you will tell her softly, He is in the pupils
> of my eyes, he is in my body and in my soul.'[34]

It is not as if the growing boy never saw his mother again. From his
exile in the servants' quarters, he would go into the *andar mahal* to
spend snatches of time with Sharada and other female residents of
the women's quarters when he was called, was sick or otherwise

in need of maternal ministrations. Here is one such memory, encapsulating the change in their relationship:

> The sky was cloudy. I was playing about in the long verandah overlooking the road. All of a sudden Satya [his sister's son, two years older than Rabi] and one of the other two boys living in the servant's quarters, for some reason I do not remember, decided to frighten me by shouting, 'Policeman! Policeman!' My ideas of the duties of policemen were of an extremely vague description. One thing I was certain about, that a person charged with a crime once placed in a policeman's hands would, as sure as a wretch caught in a crocodile's serrated grip, go under and be seen no more. Not knowing how an innocent boy could escape this relentless penal code, I bolted towards the inner apartments, with shudders running down my back for blind fear of pursuing policemen. I broke to my mother the news of my impending doom, but it did not seem to disturb her much. However, not deeming it safe to venture out again, I sat down on the sill of my mother's door to read the dog-eared Ramayana, with a marbled paper cover, which belonged to her old aunt. Alongside stretched the verandah running around the four sides of the open inner quadrangle, on which had fallen the faint afternoon glow of the clouded sky, and finding me weeping over one of its sorrowful situations my great-aunt came and took away the book from me.[35]

The shimmering mother of infancy and early childhood who illuminated the world in a dazzling, unreal light, who filled the child's inner ears with vibrations of imaginary melodies, the magician who garbed the boy in a coat of omnipotence, the sage who revealed the mystery at the fount of life, was no longer there. She had endowed Rabi with intuitive, sensual knowledge, her enduring parting gift, the ground from which Tagore could soar into his flights of creativity, the port from which he could sail onto the sea of his imagination:

> Children. . .dwell in that primal paradise where humans can obtain knowledge without wholly comprehending each step. Only when the paradise is lost comes the evil day when everything has to be understood. The road which leads to knowledge without going through the dreary process of understanding is the royal road. If that be barred, even though commerce may continue, the open sea and the mountain top cease to be possible of access.[36]

But *that* mother was gone forever. The one left behind was an ageing and often unwell Sharada whose original portrait had bled of all colour, leaving the features ashen grey, an increasingly diffuse presence destined to fade into obscurity. Rabindranath is not wholly incorrect in saying that the death of his mother did not leave a mark on him. In Rabi's psyche, his mother had died eight years earlier with his exile into the servants' quarters.

3

The Exile

Rabindranath's memories of his exile at the age of five to the children's and servants' quarters, recounted in vivid prose, and that too at a distance of seventy years (forty in *Jibansmriti*), are precise and I can do no better than, as far as possible, tell the story in his own words.

Rabi shared the exile with two other boys, his sister's son Satya and brother Soumendra, both a couple of years older than Rabi. The boys 'lived under the rule of servants. . .'

> To save themselves trouble they virtually suppressed our right of free movement. . .Going out of the house was forbidden to us, in fact we had not even the freedom of all its parts. We perforce took our peeps at nature from behind the barriers. Beyond my reach there was this limitless thing called the Outside, of which flashes and sounds and scents used momentarily to come and touch me through interstices. It seemed to want to play with me through the bars with so many gestures. But it was free and I was bound —there was no way of our meeting.[1]

Physically abused, the boys howled when they were beaten, 'which our chastisers did not consider good manners; it was in fact counted sedition against the servocracy. I cannot forget how, in order effectively to suppress such sedition, our heads used to be crammed into huge water jars then in use.'[2]

An older Rabindranath wonders why the servants were so cruel and concludes, with a hint of reproach, less towards the servants than the family caregivers, that the 'real reason must have been that the whole of our burden was thrown upon servants, and the whole burden is a thing difficult to bear even for those who are nearest and dearest. . .Of most of these tyrants of our childhood I remember only their cuffings and boxings, and nothing more.'[3]

There are two servants that stand out in Rabindranath's memory, one for his kindness and the other for his eccentricity that was, at least, not physically abusive. The first was Shyam, a dark chubby boy with long, oil-drenched locks, and a sturdy, well-built physique. 'Harshness was alien to his nature, and he was simple of heart. He had a soft corner for us young boys' . . . and would regale Rabi with stirring tales of dacoits and bandits that were as frightening as they were delightful—'How many evenings have I spent as a child, clutching my sides in terror. . .'[4] Like other servants Shyam, too, sought to restrain the growing boy's natural inclination to explore the world around him but he did this without the threat of or actual physical chastisement:

> He would put me into a selected spot and, tracing a chalk line around, warn me with solemn face and uplifted finger of the perils of transgressing this ring. Whether the threatened danger was material or spiritual I never fully understood, but a great fear used to possess me. I had read in the Ramayana of the tribulations of Sita after she left the ring drawn by Lakshman, so it was not possible for me to be skeptical of its potency.[5]

The second servant was the attendant in charge, Brajeshwar (in *Reminiscences*, Ishwar, as he was probably called by the family), a former village schoolmaster, religiously orthodox, with an obsession for cleanliness and an affected way of speaking. Rabindranath describes him as a man 'with salt-and-pepper hair and moustache, taut dry skin stretched over his face, a severe disposition, a harsh voice, and a guttural accent'.

> Deep within, he nursed a craving for food. It was not his habit to offer us full servings on our platters at mealtimes. When we sat down to eat, he would wave a luchi casually before us and ask, 'Do you want some more?' His tone would indicate the answer he wanted. 'I don't want any,' I would often reply. After that, he would not press me to have more. He also had an uncontrollable attraction for the milk bowl. A taste I did not share at all. . .In this way I had grown quite accustomed to frugal meals, right from my boyhood days. . .[6]
>
> This erstwhile schoolmaster had discovered a way of keeping us quiet in the evenings. Every evening he would gather us around the cracked castor-oil lamp and read out to us stories from the Ramayana and Mahabharata. Some of the other servants would also come and join the audience. The lamp would be throwing huge shadows right up to the beams of the roof, the little house lizards catching insects on the walls, the bats doing a mad dervish dance round and round the verandahs outside, and we listening in silent open-mouthed wonder.[7]

We must remember that it is not the factual veracity of his memories that concerns us here: whether he had sufficient food or adequate clothing—'A list of our articles of clothing, would invite a modern boy's scorn. On no pretext did we wear socks or shoes till we had passed our tenth year. In the cold weather a second cotton tunic over the first one sufficed.'[8] It is not the truth of the world but our perception of it that determines how we live in it; it is not what actually happened in the past but what we *believe* happened that shapes our responses in the present. The boy Rabi's memories of deprivation are his sensing of an inner poverty as a consequence of his exile, a depletion and 'beggaring' of the self. Rabindranath writes:

> In infancy the loving care of a woman is to be had without the asking, and, being as much a necessity as light and air, is as implicitly accepted without any conscious response: rather does the growing child often display an eagerness to free itself from the encircling web of woman's solicitude. But the unfortunate creature who is deprived of this in its proper season is beggared indeed. This had been my plight. So after being brought up in the servants' quarters when I suddenly came in for a profusion of womanly affection, I could hardly remain unconscious of it.[9]

The same caveat applies to his frequent references to his loneliness, his feeling of having been condemned to solitary confinement. Factually, of course, the family mansion—with the large extended families of his father and his uncle, not to mention a multitude of male and female servants, tutors for various subjects, visiting friends, various hangers-on and distant relatives, some of whom would stay on for months—must have been a hive of comings and goings from which Rabi could not have been completely isolated. Rabi's loneliness was not a consequence of actual isolation but a state of the soul.

As I read his recollections, I cannot but admire the creativity of the mature Rabindranath who can transform his childhood memories in a way that they both screen out and give expression to the turmoil raging in the boy Rabi's soul at the sudden banishment from the cocoon of maternal indulgence into the harshness and abuse of servocracy. Without any preparation for the transition, Rabi had to abruptly forego the gently teasing, admiring society of women and adapt to a stern and unfeeling male world of servants. Even more than the suddenness of the transition, we can sense Rabi's bewilderment and uprootedness at the contrast between an earlier, more or less unchecked benevolent indulgence and new inflexible rules governing conduct and movement that are often enforced with violence, threatened or actual.

Like many a hapless child, Rabi attempted to deal with the noxious retaliatory, violent promptings in his own soul through an imaginative displacement, turning passive into active and thus making it more bearable.

> I sometimes played the schoolmaster, with the veranda railings for pupils. They were silent with awe. There would be the occasional naughty ones, not interested in lessons at all. They would grow up to be coolies, I would warn them. Beaten black and blue, they would still show no signs of giving up their pranks. . .
>
> There was one more game I played, with Singhimama, my wooden lion. Tales of animal sacrifice performed on prayer days had convinced me that sacrificing my lion would be an event of great magnitude. Many were the blows I rained upon his neck with a twig.[10]

But even more than the violence, what grips us in his recollections are images of a small boy cut off from the riches of an animated life of a large extended family and being flung into a pit of loneliness.

> Our elders in every way kept a great distance from us, in their dress and eating, coming and going, work, conversation and amusement. We caught glimpses of all these activities, but they were beyond our reach. . .'[11]

We were too young then to take any part in these doings, but the waves of merriments and life to which they gave rise came and beat at the doors of our curiosity. . .[12]

Boys those days could take no part in adult pleasures, even from a distance. 'Go away, go away and play!' we would be told, if we plucked up the courage to go anywhere near. . .From a distance, every now and then, some snatches of it [adult entertainment] would be flung our way, like frothing foam from a waterfall. Leaning over the balcony, I would observe the scene, gazing at the dance-hall of the house opposite, sparkling with light. Outside the portico, enormous horse-drawn carriages would drive up. Some of our elder brothers would welcome the guests and escort them upstairs. . .[13]

Outside there was hustle and bustle, the sparkle of chandeliers. In my room, there was no noise at all; the brass lamp burned dimly on its stand. In the depths of my slumber, I could hear the clash of cymbals every time the *taal*, the rhythm-cycle of the dance, reached the point of climax called the *sam*.[14]

The intensity of Rabi's longing for the inner apartments, the 'Elysium of my imagination. . .abode of all freedom', whose 'secluded leisure had something mysterious about it'[15] and the complex emotions associated with the exile, come through in a memory that has the feel of a screen memory. Screen memory in psychoanalysis refers to a seemingly innocuous childhood memory that is a displaced reference to a forgotten but truly significant aspect of childhood, which is retained into adult life and frequently reactivated in times of stress.

A murky flickering lantern is hanging in the long venetian-screened corridor leading from the outer to the inner apartments. At its end this passage becomes a flight of four or five steps, which light does not reach, and down which I pass into the galleries running round the first inner quadrangle. A shaft of moonlight slants from the eastern sky into the western angle of these verandahs, leaving the rest in darkness. In this patch of light the maids have gathered and are squatting close together, with legs outstretched, rolling cotton waste into lamp-wicks, and chatting in undertones of their village homes.[16]

This picture, which Rabindranath says is one of many others from that period that is 'indelibly printed' on his mind, has all the well-known qualities of screen memories: external brilliance, preponderance of the visual, and a notion of the self as an onlooker. That there are turbulent emotions lurking under the apparent serenity of the scene is attested to by the fact that Rabi was a timid boy, terrified of the demonic spirits that roamed the house at night, and would not have dreamt of venturing into the inner apartments by traversing the connecting passage.

The narrow passage from the public area to the inner quarters of the house was screened by Venetian blinds, and lit by dim lanterns suspended above. Crossing it, I felt sure I was being followed. A shiver would run down my spine. . .Every so often, the nasal wail of the shankchunni, the nocturnal spirit, would cause some maid servant to collapse in a fainting fit. That female ghost was the most temperamental of all, and she had a weakness for fish. There was also an unknown standing figure, straddling the dense almond tree to the west of the house, and the third floor cornice. . .When my elder brother's friend laughed off the matter, the servants of the house were convinced that he knew nothing about religious faith. Just wait till the spirit wrung his neck one day, that would put an end to all his learned wisdom . . .Inside a dark chamber on the ground floor, in row upon row of enormous water vessels, the year's supply of drinking water would be stored. It was a well-known fact that the spirits who secretly inhabited those damp, gloomy spaces on the lower floor had huge, gaping mouths, eyes in their chests, ears like kulos—the flat U-shaped baskets used for husking rice—and feet that faced the wrong way. As I crossed those ghostly shadows to reach the private garden of the house, my heart would heave in terror, adding wings to my feet.[17]

As we shall see later, in old age and at a time of physical illness and psychological vulnerability, these childhood apparitions, escaping conscious control, resurfaced in the drawings of his *Puravi* poems.

Hidden behind the screen of the otherwise innocuous memory is not only an intense longing to return 'home' to the maternal-feminine world of infancy and early childhood, to undo the separation, but also a reproof against the mother who is held responsible for imposing the exile. Because of the disturbance it will create in an idealized mother image and the mother–son bond, this reproach—and I am speculating here—is buried in the deeper layers of the psyche, accessible only in Rabindranath's creative oeuvre rather than in his conscious memories. Two short stories, *The Homecoming* and *The Postmaster* are vivid examples of this troubling, and troubled, dynamic in the mother–son relationship.

In *The Homecoming*, the fourteen-year-old Phatik is sent away by his widowed mother to live with his uncle and his family in Calcutta where he goes to school. The boy is lonely, homesick for the life of his village, and desperately yearns for his mother.

A kind of physical love like that of animals; a longing to be in the presence of one who is loved; an inexpressible wistfulness during absence; a silent cry of the inmost heart for the mother, like the lowing of a calf on the twilight; this love, which was almost an animal instinct, agitated the shy, nervous, lean, uncouth and ugly boy. No one could understand it, but it preyed upon his mind continually.[18]

Every day he asks his uncle when the school holidays will begin when he can return to his village home. Treated badly by the aunt, Phatik runs away but is brought back, suffering from high fever. The mother is called from the village to be at the bedside of her dying son. In the last scene of the story:

> Phatik stopped his restless movements for a moment. His hands ceased beating up and down. He said: 'Eh?'
> The mother cried again: 'Phatik, my darling, my darling.'
> Phatik very slowly turned his head and, without seeing anybody, said: 'Mother, the holidays have come.'[19]

In the second, *The Postmaster*, together with *The Kabuliwala*, perhaps one of Rabindranath's best realized short fictions, a postmaster from Calcutta is transferred to a remote village. Lonely in his new surroundings, the postmaster starts paying a good deal of attention to Ratan, an orphaned little village girl who serves him. They develop a close relationship. He teaches her to read and write and in the evenings shows interest in the events of her life while also talking to her of his memories of his own home and family, drawing the girl closer and closer.

Then, one day, unsuccessful in his efforts to be transferred back to Calcutta, the postmaster resigns his job and decides to return to the big city. Busy in preparations for his eagerly awaited return to 'civilization', the postmaster is insensible to the heartbreak of the little girl. At the end of the story, only when he is in the boat:

> The postmaster felt a huge anguish: the image of a simple young village-girl's grief-stricken face seemed to speak a great inarticulate

universal sorrow. He felt a sharp desire to go back: should he not fetch that orphaned girl, whom the world had abandoned? But the wind was filling the sails by then, the swollen river was flowing fiercely, the village had been left behind, the riverside burning-ground was in view. Detached by the current of the river, he reflected philosophically that in life there are many separations, many deaths. What point was there in going back? Who belonged to whom in this world?

But Ratan had no such philosophy to console her. All she could do was wander near the post office, weeping copiously. Maybe a faint hope lingered in her mind that Dadababu might return; and this was enough to tie her to the spot, prevent her from going far. O poor, unthinking human heart! Error will not go away, logic and reason are slow to penetrate. We cling fast with both arms to hope, refusing to believe the weightiest proofs against it, embracing it with all our strength. In the end it escapes, ripping our veins and draining our hearts' blood; until, regaining consciousness, we rush to fall into snares of delusion all over again.[20]

Parenthetically, let me note here that Rabindranath is also endorsing the psychoanalytic concept of 'repetition compulsion', that we are fated to repeat the fundamental themes of our lives over and over again; but, then, the poets have always known the deeper secrets of the human heart earlier and better than the analysts.

The child's abandonment by the mother—let us not be led astray by the masks of different genders worn by the protagonists in *The Postmaster*, a tactic that is common in the construction of dreams—and the consoling fantasy of the repentant mother suffering for this deed, is the major theme of both the stories. There are, of course, minor differences in the emphasis between the two: the caregiver's anguish is more dramatic (and hence more satisfying for the child) in *The Homecoming* and is but short-lived in *The Postmaster* where it is soon overcome through philosophical reflection; the abandonment follows a more explicit seduction of the child into the caregiver's world in *The Postmaster,* flagging the motif of 'seduction and betrayal'. It is through the medium of fiction that an older Rabindranath revisits six-year-old Rabi's reproach against his mother of having first seduced the child into an intimacy beyond compare, her maternal presence imbuing the world with enchantment, and then of having abandoned him, a grievance that is permeated with quiet despair more than an overt anger. The intervening years and the medium of fiction now allow the writer to lay on an authentic colour of anguish with the brush of unconscious memory. Just as good poetry (or fiction) does not come into existence if the writer is too near the feeling to which he is giving expression—'Nearness has too much of the compelling about it and the imagination is not sufficiently free unless it can get away from its influence'[21]—so also can the writer never describe a feeling from which he is too distant with any degree of conviction. In other words, I cannot *authentically* express and convey an emotion I have never experienced, even if minimally, myself.

Like many children, Rabi's initial efforts at dealing with his loneliness, a dysphoric state of the mind, is by an imaginative use of a material object: his grandmother's discarded palki—palanquin—lying abandoned in a corner of the empty ledger room in the children and servants' quarters.

> All around us was the hustle and bustle of male and female attendants deployed in different quarters of the house. I was about seven or eight. I had no useful role to play in the world; and that old palki, too, had been dismissed from all forms of useful employment. That was why I felt such a deep affinity with it. As if it was an island in the sea, and on holidays, I was Robinson Crusoe, lost to the world, concealed behind the palki's closed doors, to elude the oppressive surveillance. . .

As time advanced, the sunlight grew harsh, the bell in the portico announced the time; but inside the palki, the day refused to keep track of the passing hours. In there, it was the noontime of those bygone days, when the danka, the large kettledrum at the palace gate, would signal the end of the public audience, and the king would depart for his daily bath in sandalwood-scented water. One afternoon, on a holiday, my supervisors had dozed off after their daytime meal. I was alone. The immobile palki sped through the terrain of my mind, borne by loyal minions made of air...to faraway lands bearing names gleaned from books...Then, at some other point, the palki transformed into *mayurpankhi*, a magical boat shaped like a peacock.[22]

Imagination, and one of its chief products, fantasy, which has been called 'vehicle of hope, healer of trauma, protector from reality, concealer of truth, fixer of identity, restorer of tranquility, enemy of fear and sadness, cleanser of the soul',[23] is the inheritance of every child even when it is more lively in some children than others. Rabi's vivid imagination does its assigned task in propelling his fantasies beyond prosaic reality to elevate him to the position of a king served by minions rather than being a helpless child at the mercy of servocracy, lends wings to the boy chafing at the restrictions on his movement to venture into far-off lands. Rabi, however, went on to develop a rarer kind of imagination that is more mysterious than the normal consolatory one most of us are familiar with, an imagination that is not the offspring of an encounter between our wishes and an implacable reality but goes well beyond a dramatization of our desires. I have called this imagination—which is not only the basis of much great art and some visions of science and philosophy but is also the underlying principle of many religious rituals and spiritual disciplines—*connective* imagination.[24] Although it shares with normal imagination the ability to make images and the capacity to access and elaborate on early memories, connective imagination is markedly less self-centred, its imaginative process characterized by a deep affinity and an intimate connection between the knower and the known which, at times, can extend to a union of the two. Often assigned a 'spiritual' origin because of its latter characteristic, it is to the appearance of connective imagination and its power to transform anxious loneliness into creative solitude in Rabi's childhood to which we now turn. His loneliness, though an imposed fate at the beginning of the exile, would often be transformed into what the psychoanalyst D.W. Winnicott has called the capacity to be alone in the presence of others,[25] a highly valuable human attribute, and not only for creative people. Most people fear solitude, confusing it with loneliness and its associated absences and silences, and seek to avoid being alone by fretfully seeking the company of other people or, in their absence, by hours of internet surfing or television watching. As Kierkegaard has put it, '. . .one does everything possible by way of diversions and the Janizary music of loud-voiced enterprises to keep lonely thoughts away. . .'[26] Solitude is not seclusion, the absence of other people in no way a reflection of an inner emptiness but of a fullness, of an overflowing, its silence resounding with a myriad voices. The prototype of this sense of solitude is the infant's experience of being alone with the mother as she goes about her tasks, perhaps humming to herself, as her presence gradually builds itself into the infant's psyche. Rabindranath's *My Song* will have a special resonance for those fortunate enough to be blessed with a sense of this secure presence that might dim at times but never completely disappears.

This song of mine will wind its music around you, my child, like the fond arms of love.
This song of mine will touch your forehead like a kiss of blessing.
When you are alone it will sit by your side and whisper in your ear, when you are in the crowd it will fence you about with aloofness.

My song will be like a pair of wings to your dreams, it will transport your heart to the verge of the unknown.

It will be like the faithful star overhead when dark night is over your road.

My song will sit in the pupils of your eyes, and will carry your sight into the heart of things.

And when my voice is silent in death, my song will speak in your living heart.[27]

It may well be, as the psychoanalyst Frieda Fromm-Reichman has observed, that 'only the creative person who is not afraid of this constructive aloneness [solitude in our parlance] will have free command over his creativity'.[28]

Rabindranath, like no other writer, has explored the tension between loneliness and solitude in his own life: the one with a feeling of emptiness and being deserted, vulnerable to depression, the other with a feeling of fullness and constant presence of loved others even if they are long gone or physically absent. In life, as distinct from thought, the distinctions between being lonely and being solitary are not as clear-cut; there is an inevitable messiness where the two intersect and where the one changes into the other. Rabindranath was quite clear about solitude lying at the foundation of his psyche and his work. In a letter to C.F. Andrews, one of the very few people with whom Rabindranath sought some degree of intimacy in his late adulthood (unlike most people, he had no friends from his youth), he writes:

During the most part of my life my mind has been made accustomed to travel the inner path of dreams till it has lost all confidence in its power to thread its way through the zigzags of the outer world. In fact its attention has never been trained to accept the miscellaneous responsibilities of the clamorous surface life of society.[29]

Like the poet Rilke who welcomed solitude where he could be in his work 'like a pit in its fruit', Rabindranath writes in another letter, 'All through my life I have ever worked alone, for my life and work have ever been one; I am like the tree which builds up its timber by its own inner living process—and therefore it needs leisure and space, sunlight and air.'[30]

He was also cognizant of the distinction between being alone and being solitary and that the latter needed a harmonious presence of the mental representations of lost loved ones in one's psyche: 'Wherever there is creation, man has to be alone. By merging the "many" within the "one", one has to be alone. But if this does not merge then the creator cannot be alone. Then crowd makes chaos.'[31]

Whenever Rabindranath felt lonely, his life 'burdened with responsibilities too heavy for a single man to bear' and 'stranded in a desolation where every individual has to struggle through his own problems unaided', it was his inner solitude that came to his rescue and he 'felt again the current turn inward from the world to my soul. It is the floodtide of life and companionship, it sweeps my burdens off my shoulders and carries me along with it in its joyous course.'[32] Solitude was not only creative but also curative, the one merging into the other.

Yet, even for the most self-sufficient solitary person, some direct connection with other human beings is a necessity. This is especially true for those whose work is centred around people and not phenomena of nature or abstractions of thought. The fences Rabindranath put around himself as an adult continue the theme of the confining chalk circle drawn around him as a child. The difference is that what was then passively endured is now actively chosen as an adult. Rabindranath would be the master of his isolation; yet the occasional (and inevitable) shortcomings in reaching this goal would renew an old suffering and victimhood.

Here I must add that the creative solitude Rabindranath's soul is fretting for, where one withdraws from the world with imagination as one's sole companion, is hazardous if such a withdrawal is not an act of choice but imposed, in the sense that it is a consequence of intercourse with the world that one has found too painful. The danger then is not finding the healing balm of solitude but the cold desert of loneliness, which many creative individuals seek to make bearable by narcissistic self-aggrandizement and a sense of grandiosity that spurns all human contact. Much like the patient who, when asked why he stays closeted in his room, compulsively masturbating, replies, 'But, doctor, that is where one meets the best people!' Rabindranath's own view of his loneliness is characterized not by self-aggrandizement, but, most of the time, by self-abnegation, his inability to form attachments a flaw in his character that sets him apart but not above other human beings. He wrote in 1894 to his niece Indira Devi:

> I feel ashamed to admit, and sad to think—that usually I feel very distressed with human company. I feel pain inside—every day I advise myself to be like others, mix with people with ease, to enjoy life's pleasures with ease like others—but all along I have always had such a strange boundary which I have never been able to transgress. Among people I am like a new being, it has never been possible for me to connect with them completely—I have been far away from even those who have been my old friends. When I am so distant by nature, then naturally to be close just because of social norms is very strenuous for the mind. Yet to remain disconnected with people is not completely natural to me—every now and then

I feel compelled to be amidst them—the conflicts with people for
the sake of life-force are equally important.[33]

However bracing the air at the higher reaches of creative solitude,
frequent descents into the plains of everyday living are unavoidable.
In the plains, it is the myriad social interactions—the warmth of
companionship, the pleasures of friendship and the deep satisfactions
of intimacy in the family—that give life much of its meaning. And
as one ages and the creative fire burns less bright than it did in
the fullness of youth or even in the autumn of the middle years,
the sojourns in the plains get longer and longer. It is now that life
makes unfamiliar demands on those, like Rabindranath, who never
sufficiently developed the art of living in the intermediate space
between loneliness and solitude, who missed out on the more muted
palette of colours that lie between those expressing the anguish of
the former and the exultation of the latter.

The old poet would seek to fill the vacuum left by the desertion of
his Muse by seeking company but knew that this was not a solution
for his malaise. In a letter to Rani Mahalanobis, a forty-years-younger
woman friend and a confidante of his old age, there is a tone of
regret when he writes:

I have remained alone in my load of work. This loneliness is
not very pleasant for me because that work which is for people
is fundamentally against being alone—for that work it is very
necessary to be connected with people. But I did not have much
of what could attract people to me—yet the work which I am
carrying along all these long years, my thoughts about it alone
have kept pushing me ahead.[34]

There are intimations of a quiet despair as the aged poet seeks to
reverse a lifelong yearning for solitude and enter the ordinary world

of human commerce but, failing, again seeks to reconnect to his familiar 'life-force', his Jibandevata—the Entheos, the god-within.

> Don't know when along with my weak body my internal light started fading, that's when I started losing my strength to gather company within myself. From that time I took interest in external company. But perhaps my true nature is of solitude—the impact of company does not give it any strength but rather makes it lazy. And in that whirlpool of laziness everything that is great gets drawn in—and from there comes tiredness. Till now, whatever strength I have gathered, whatever I have learnt, all has been by being alone within myself. I have always been a run-away-boy from school—whenever I have hesitated hearing the call of the solitary sky, whenever I have stepped back instead of leaping forward, there was danger. That call has reached my ears today—in the shelter of my ripe age I am searching for that path.[35]

As Rabindranath aged, he became more and more aware of the icy fingers of loneliness that would often grip his heart. What he would then pine for was simple human warmth, a feeling of being lovingly connected with another human being, even if the connection was not intellectually or otherwise stimulating. In another letter to Rani, six years before his death, he writes:

> Bouma [son's wife] came yesterday. When she was not there, going home was distasteful. Youth seems to return with old age. Have spent so many years alone, have never thought of this before, but these days my mind searches for my mother. My heart yearns for caring lately—if I can't find someone on whose caring I can depend on it seems like I am not grounded, but a flying balloon. This is the curse of old age; have to keep looking for strength from others, company of others. . .[36]

But to return to the beginning of it all: how the five-year-old Rabi—exiled from the inner quarters of the women and forbidden to enter those of the men—struggles to pull himself out from the pit of loneliness as a matter of simple psychological survival, and finds the door into a solitude that will be the soil for the flowering of his creativity, a transformation that is perhaps a key to Rabindranath's creative genius, is a subject I shall explore in the next chapter.

4

The Terrace and the Inner Garden

In the afternoons, while the servants dozed after lunch—their stomachs full, their surveillance considerably relaxed if not totally absent—Rabi would often sneak up the stairs to the terrace of the inner apartments. 'In my life, that open terrace was the main area of freedom. On that terrace, from infancy to adulthood, I passed my days—all sorts of days, spent in all sorts of ways.'[1] Here, high above the ground on the empty terrace,

I would stand and gaze. . . My glance first falls on the row of coconut trees at the further edge of our inner garden. Through these are seen the 'Singhi's Garden' with its cluster of huts and its tank, and on the edge of the tank the dairy of our milk-woman, Tara: still further on, mixed up with the tree-tops, the various shapes and different heights of the terraced roofs of Calcutta flashing back the blazing whiteness of the midday sun, stretch right away into the grayish blue of the eastern horizon. And some of these far distant dwellings from which stand forth their roofed stairways leading up to the terrace, look as if with uplifted finger and a wink they are hinting to me of the mysteries of their interiors. Like the beggar at the palace door imagines impossible

treasures to be held in its strong-rooms closed to him, I can hardly
tell of the wealth of play and freedom these unknown dwellings
seem to me crowded with.'[2]

In his *Boyhood Days*, Rabindranath emphasizes the terrace's female
character.

> This terrace, above the private quarters of the house, belonged
> entirely to women. The place was well in tune with the demands
> of the larder. It received direct sunlight, which facilitated the
> pickling of lemons. There, the women, their brass vessels full of
> ground black gram, squeezed out drops of the mixture to form
> baris, while they dried their hair in the open. The female attendants
> would hang out the washing in the sun.[3]

Rabindranath's further description of women's activities on the
terrace is as true of many well-to-do households all over India today,
especially in villages and provincial towns, as it was then, more than
a hundred and fifty years ago. Indeed, he evokes for me similar scenes
from my own childhood in the 1940s in the Punjab, at the other end
of the subcontinent, though the pickle in ceramic jars that would be
maturing in the sun on our terrace would not be of tender jackfruit,
steeped in mustard oil, but of turnip and cauliflower.

The terrace, though, is more than a symbol of the lost maternal-
feminine universe of infancy and Rabi's climbing to it most afternoons
is not only an attempt at an unconscious emotional refuelling. The
paragraphs in his reminiscences establishing the terrace's femininity
are immediately followed by musings on an absent father who was
constantly travelling and rarely at home.

> When my father was home, he would occupy the room on the
> second floor. Concealed behind the attic, I would often watch him

from afar, as he meditated silently before sunrise. Hands folded
on his lap, like a white stone statue on the terrace. Sometimes,
he would depart for the hills, and be away for many days. Then
visiting that terrace gave me the thrill of high adventure, like
crossing the seven seas. . .Sliding my hand through the shutter
slats, I would unlatch the door to the [father's] bedroom. Directly
facing the door was a sofa; where I would ensconce myself, feeling
utterly alone. The watchmen authorized to hold me captive were
drowsy, their stomachs full; stretching and yawning, they lay
sprawled across their floor mats. . .[4]

The boy would then turn on the faucet in his father's bathroom and
splash running water all over his body.

Drying my body with a bed sheet, I would feel very relaxed. In
no time at all, my period of leisure would be over. The bell in the
portico announced four o'clock. . .Downstairs, by now, they would
be searching for the boy who had eluded his captors.[5]

We can sense that for Rabi the empty terrace lying forlorn in
the afternoon sun is not a desert of loneliness but an expanse of
solitude where he feels singularly peaceful, serene and, above all,
free. The terrace was both a defence against the almost unbearable
anguish of exile and a site for providing vital nutrients for developing
Rabi's capacity for solitude, for knowing, appreciating and joyfully
accepting to be alone, an ability which some have held to be sine qua
non for one who would be a poet.[6] A sense of the poet's solitude,
or of loneliness seeking to transform itself into the former, is often
our most dominant impression in reading poetry. This is also true of
Rabindranath's poetry, especially at times of psychological crises in
his life where many poems highlight his struggle to turn loneliness
into solitude, very often through the evocation of the loved one's

sensual presence. One such example, among many, is the poem 'Fruit Gathering', published in 1916, a year after a major depressive episode.

> When the weariness of the road is upon me, and the thirst of the sultry day; when the ghostly hours of the dusk throw their shadows across my life, then I cry not for your voice only, my friend, but for your touch.
>
> There is anguish in my heart for the burden of its riches not given to you.
>
> Put your hand through the night, let me hold it and keep it; let me feel its touch along the lengthening stretch of my loneliness.[7]

The terrace, then, combines Rabi's longing for a reimmersion in the inner sanctum of the mother with his yearning to venture out into the great outer world represented by the father. Solitude, which some analysts following Winnicott believe is an access to the maternal presence while being alone, may be a necessary precondition for creativity. Yet in Rabindranath's case solitude gives birth to creative works only if it is also impregnated by the paternal principle, represented in Rabi's life by his father Debendranath who embodies the immense spaces of the outside world and especially the soaring peaks of the Himalayas straining towards the sky to which Debendranath was persistently drawn.

This urge to bring together dualities of the maternal and the paternal, male and female, inside and outside—*ghare baire*[8]—will extend to other dualities—India–West, human–divine, the works of man and the inspiration of nature—and is a singular feature of Rabindranath's literary oeuvre and philosophical writings. If there is one creative genius who bears witness to Jung's observation that 'Every creative person is a duality or a synthesis of contradictory aptitudes',[9] it is Rabindranath. What is important to note is that for him the bringing together of dualities is not in the sense of seeking their impossible union but their harmony. In other words, creativity is born from the harmony of conflicting and contrary forces.

The tension between the dualities in his psyche and his striving to produce harmony among them, I believe, is the motor of Rabindranath's poetry and art. In a letter to C.F. Andrews, perhaps his closest friend—or as close as he could get to any other human being—he writes:

> I have one principle to guide my thoughts in most things of vital importance—and it is this: that the figure that represents creation is not 1 but 2. In the harmony of two contradictory forces everything rests. Whenever our logic tries to simplify things by reducing the troublesome two into one it goes wrong. . . truth is beyond logic, it is the everlasting miracle, it is static and dynamic at the same time, it is ideal and real, it is finite and infinite.

Contradictions may seem to hurt each other 'like the finger and the string but this contradiction produces music; when only one predominates there is the sterility of silence.'[10]

Many men and women who have a secure maternal presence within have welcomed solitude. For solitude to be *creative*, more is needed. The necessary foundation of solitude requires a superstructure of tension between dualities and a striving for their harmony. The harmony, too, is not a one-time achievement but a continuous process that may, and often does, go off the rails. The rapturous feeling that arises when the effort is successful is beyond compare yet doomed to be evanescent.

Rabindranath is well aware of some of his own dualities, for instance of his conflict between wanting to reach out to others and a hankering for solitude, between venturing out and withdrawal, of a restlessness that sets him off on travels to distant parts of the world, meeting people, and then bemoaning that all he ever wants is to be alone in his secluded village home. A dwelling in solitude, he says at one place, is destructive since solitude needs nourishment from the world if it is not to be gravely depleted.

> Man is overcome by profound depression while nodding through his voluptuously lazy hours of seclusion, because in this way he is deprived of full commerce with life. Such is the despondency from which I have always painfully struggled to get free. . .I strained with the same yearning towards the world of man in my youth, as I did in my childhood towards outside nature from within the chalk-ring drawn around me by the servants. How rare, how unattainable, how far away it seemed! And yet if we cannot get in touch with it, if from it no breeze can blow, no current come, if no road be there for free goings and comings of travellers, then the dead things that accumulate around us never get removed but continue to be heaped up till they smother all life.[11]

Yet, at another place, his cry for solitude, to be shielded from commerce with other people, is equally heartfelt:

> I do not want to wander about anymore. I am pining for a corner in which to nestle down snugly, away from the crowd. . .I hanker after a corner because it serves to bring calmness to my mind. . .If it is allowed a little leisurely solitude, and can look about and think to its heart's content, it will express its feelings to its satisfaction.
>
> This freedom of solitude is what my mind is fretting for; it would be alone with its imaginings, as the creator broods over his own creation.[12]

The complaint of normal human relationships as being destructive of creativity has also been made by other creative geniuses. The philosopher Nietzsche writes that he goes into solitude 'so as not to drink out of everybody's cistern. When I am among the many I live as the many do, and I do not think as I really think; after a time it always seems as if they want to banish me from myself and rob me of my soul.'[13]

The other place where the child's solitude—not in the sense of loneliness or a self-centred withdrawal—flowered was the inner garden of the Tagore house. The garden, a mere patch of green, consisted of little else than

> A citron tree, a couple of plum trees of different varieties, and a row of coconut trees. In the centre was a paved circle, the cracks of which various grasses and weeds had invaded and planted in the victorious standards. Only those flowering plants which refused to die of neglect continued uncomplainingly to perform their respective duties. . .
>
> None the less, I suspect that Adam's Garden of Eden could hardly have been better adorned than this one of ours. . .Our inner garden was my paradise; it was enough for me. I well remember how in the early autumn dawn I would run there as soon as I was awake. A scent of dewy grass and foliage would rush to meet me, and the morning with its cool fresh sunlight would peep out at me over the top of the Eastern garden wall from below the trembling tassels of the coconut palms.[14]

The row of coconut trees, to which he often returns in his writings and letters, were to him both a symbol of the fullness of those childhood moments of solitude and of the 'spiritual' origins of his creativity which has come to be viewed as the hallmark of his art, poetry and philosophy.

> I remember, when I was a child, that a row of coconut trees by our garden wall, with their branches beckoning the rising

sun on the horizon, gave me a companionship as living as I was myself. I know it was my imagination which transmuted the world around me into my own world—the imagination which seeks unity, which deals with it. But we have to consider that the companionship was true; that the universe in which I was born had in it an element profoundly akin to my own imaginative mind, one which wakens in all children's natures the Creator, whose pleasure is in interweaving the web of creation with His own patterns of many-coloured strands. It is something akin to us, and therefore harmonious to our imagination. When we find some strings vibrating in unison with others, we know that this sympathy carries in it an eternal reality. The fact that the world stirs our imagination in sympathy tells us that this creative imagination is a common truth both in us and in the heart of existence.[15]

The spiritual origins of Rabindranath's creativity—to which I will return in the concluding chapter—are not the central concern of this book that focuses more on its psychological underpinnings. And this in spite of Rabindranath himself who unequivocally attributes his poetic and artistic creativity to a transcendent 'spirit', a deep-lying continuous medium that connects all human minds with each other and with the universe.[16] To continue in my biographical mode, one could say that the *psychological* origins of Rabindranath's 'creative imagination' can be traced back to a traumatic separation from the mother. We see this clearly in the poem 'Mone Pora' (I Cannot Remember):

I cannot remember my mother,
only sometimes in the midst of my play
a tune seems to hover over my playthings,
the tune of some song that she used to hum while
rocking my cradle.

I cannot remember my mother,
but when in the early autumn morning
the smell of the *shiuli* flowers floats in the air
the scent of the morning service in the temple comes
to me as the scent of my mother.

I cannot remember my mother,
only when from my bedroom window
I send my eyes into the blue of the distant sky
I feel that the stillness of my mother's gazing on my
face has spread all over the sky.[17]

In stanza one, Rabindranath is the recipient of his mother's auditory and kinaesthetic nearness; in stanza two, of her scent. In stanza three, animated by the sensual immersion into the maternal, the poet sends his eyes outward, beyond the confining home, initiating a cosmic mother looking at his face.[18] Underneath the experience that created the poem, a psychoanalyst would speculate, there is the fantasy of continuously being watched over by his dead mother, although like all works of literary and artistic creativity, the poem itself, as we shall see in the last chapter, is not merely a compensation for or even sublimation of the loss.

The mere linking, however careful, of Rabindranath's poetic imagination to the experience of early childhood loss would be reflexively damned by some as 'reductionist'. And, indeed, what Erik Erikson called 'the originological fallacy',[19] the psychoanalytic habit of finding the causes of a man's *whole* development in his childhood conflicts, is as pernicious as teleology wherein ends are supposed to explain complex early developments. Yet, the mere tracing of a phenomenon to its origins is not a fallacy as long as other, later contributions are also given their due; the tracing of a river to its source is not to deny that there are other streams that flow into its course as it meanders from its origins into the sea. I believe Rabindranath would have agreed.

> When in later life, I wandered about like a madcap, at the first coming of spring with a handful of half-blown jasmines tied in a corner of my muslin scarf, as I stroked my forehead with the soft, rounded, tapering buds, the touch of my mother's fingers would come back to me; and I clearly realized that the tenderness that dwelt in the tips of those lovely fingers was the very same as that which blossoms every day in the purity of these jasmine buds; and that whether we know it or not, this tenderness is on the earth in boundless measure.[20]

In the above quote, Rabindranath is not reducing creative imagination to a wish for reconnection with the mother of his infancy but imbuing the universe itself with a beneficent maternal spirit. In his compelling, poetic description, he also shows that though the maternal origins of his creative imagination are visible and continue to influence the phenomenon, they do so in a highly modified and complex way.

The solitude in which the dualities have been brought together in harmony and given birth to a creative imagination will be invariably lost time and again during a long life when the reproaches, loneliness and despair of the mourning child would re-emerge and temporarily overwhelm the poet's psyche. At such times the terrace and the inner garden would lose their magic and mystery, their symbolic riches and transformative power, become ordinary spaces in a now crumbling mansion that has seen its best days: a half-forgotten flat expanse of a roof and a neglected patch of land with a few shrubs and trees. To restore his psychic equilibrium, Rabindranath would mourn their loss and seek to conjure up their images from the memories of his childhood. Thus, for instance, returning from a long sojourn

in the West and on board the ship bound for India he writes to
Andrews:

> The rude handling by the sea does not affect me much, but the
> gloom and unrest and the tremendous rise and fall of waves like
> a giant's beating of the breast in despair depress my mind. The
> sad thought very often comes to me with imaginary supposition
> that I may never reach the Indian shore and my heart aches with
> a longing to see the arms of my motherland extended into the
> sea with the palm leaves rustling in the air. It is the land where I
> first gazed in the eyes of my first great sweetheart—my Muse—
> who made me love the sunlight touching the top of the coconut
> row through a pale mist of severe autumn morning and the
> storm laden rain clouds rolling up from some abyss behind the
> horizon, carrying in their dark folds a thrilling expectation of a
> mad outburst of showers.[21]

The terrace and the garden, then, are the primary settings of
Rabindranath's inner theatre; their loss, recovery and reclamation,
constitute a vital repetitive theme in his inner life and work. A
symbolic reconnecting with these sets of his inner theatre in his
poetry (and in old age, in paintings) was indispensable for establishing
harmony among the divisions and dualities in his self through
what has been called the 'curious clarity of poetry'.[22] He seems to
be aware of this theme when, in another context, he writes, 'Thus
did the First Book of my life come to an end with these chapters of
union, separation and reunion. Or rather, it is not true to say it has
come to an end. The same subject has still to be continued through
elaborate solutions of worse complexities, to a greater conclusion.'[23]
He leaves the reader wondering whether the observations are about
his first book of poems, *Morning Songs,* or the first book of his life—
childhood.

5

A Painful Welcome to the World

Rabi's school years, which began when he was seven years old were, to put it mildly, trying. The systematic instruction that a child must be exposed to during these years—demanding that he learn to obtain satisfaction from completion of work, however tedious he may find it, or discover pleasure in the virtues of paying steady attention and persevering diligence—were a daytime nightmare for a boy like Rabi whose soul had been crying for freedom from the regimentation of servocracy and for exciting encounters with the outside world that would fire his imagination, not dim its glow.

All that his entry into the life of the wider world brought him was a phalanx of private tutors and schoolteachers who, with a couple of exceptions, he experienced as enemies of his dearest possession and indispensable ally in the preservation of his psychic well-being: his imagination. It was this intangible realm of symbols and metaphors, of tangled emotions, fleeting impressions and vivid dreams, with an empathetic connection to the not-self, especially nature, which Rabindranath always acknowledged as both the guardian and the source of his creativity. For instance, talking of one of his dreams that later became a short story, *Rajarshi* (The Royal Sage), he writes,

'Many of my stories have come to me in my dreams—and other writings too.'[1] Whereas the fount of his imagination, solitude, had earlier been threatened by the dysphoria of loneliness, it was now in danger of being encroached upon and indeed swamped by a horde of squatters that were his lot during the school years. And though Rabindranath's recollections of this period are laced with wit, the bouts of discouragement, if not despair, that Rabi felt during these years manages to seep through the mature defence of humour which Rabindranath employs in the telling of the story.

Rabi's day began at dawn with the practice of wrestling grips under the tutelage of a blind wrestler, Kana Pehlwan.

> Returning from the wrestling ring, I would find a student from the medical college waiting to teach me all about human bones. Suspended on the wall was a complete human skeleton. There it hung, on our bedroom wall at night, the bones rattling in the breeze. . .
>
> The bell in the portico announced seven o'clock. Tutor Nilkamal arrived on the dot, there was no question of a minute's delay. He had a thin, emaciated body, but his health, like his pupil's, never failed, not once did he complain of a headache. I would go to the table, books and slate in hand. On the blackboard, chalk marks, all in Bengali, would inscribe the mathematical signs of arithmetic, geometry, algebra.[2]

Nilkamal Babu was followed by the second tutor, of Sanskrit, and Rabi had to learn the Sanskrit grammar book *Mugabodh* by heart, 'without understanding a word of it'.

> The heavier the daylong pressure of learning a variety of subjects, the harder my mind would endeavour to secretly discard some of its weight. The knowledge learned by rote would struggle for

loopholes to escape the net, and the tutor Nilkamal's opinion of his pupil's caliber was not worth announcing to all and sundry. . .

The sun climbed the sky, casting half the courtyard in shade. Nine o'clock. Short, dark-skinned Gobindo, dirty yellow gamcha on his shoulder, would escort me to my bath. Sharp at nine-thirty, we were served our fixed portions of the routine menu: dal, rice and machher jhol, fish cooked in gravy. I had no taste for it.[3]

At ten, it was time for school, 'my own Andamans, my place of exile from ten to four' and as Rabi was driven away in a palki carriage hauled by the old horse, he would wistfully look up at the terrace of a house at the end of the alley where two small girls, unmindful of the time, played with cowries while their mother dried her long damp hair in the sun. 'Girls did not have to hurry to school, those days. It seemed so fortunate to be born a girl!'[4]

Rabi would return from school after four-thirty when his gymnastics trainer would be waiting. As soon as he left, the art teacher would appear. And as the evening began to turn into night and oil lamps were lit, the day's final and greatest torment was heralded with the appearance of Aghor Babu, a medical student who tutored Rabi in English.

'Our bodies were weary at the end of the day, and our minds yearned for the inner apartments. The book was black and thick with difficult words, and the subject matter could hardly have been less inviting, for it contained none of Saraswati, goddess of learning's maternal tenderness.'[5]

The English reader 'with its dark jacket, seemed to crouch on the table, waiting to pounce'.

The cover was loose, the pages torn and stained; in the wrong places I had honed my writing skills, inscribing my name in English, all in capital letters. As I read, I dozed off; every now and then, I would start into wakefulness. The time I spent not reading far exceeded the hours I devoted to studying.[6]

Neither sprinkling water into the eyes, nor taking a run around the verandahs nor the tutor's attempt at shaming Rabi by comparing him to some of his other brilliant pupils, helped to alleviate the torture of the English lessons. It was only in bed that Rabi finally found refuge from the relentless encroachments of the day and could deliver himself into the soothing embrace of his imagination, 'There, I listened to the story that never reached its conclusion: "The prince rides across the boundless terrain. . ."'[7]

An older Rabindranath concedes that not all his tutors were imagination's enemies. Rabi eagerly looked forward to the Sunday demonstrations of physical science by the science tutor and the feelings of wonder that filled him as he watched simple experiments in physics. Even Aghor Babu, the medical student who taught him English, was an enthusiastic young man who sought to enliven his lessons by acquainting his young charge with the mysteries of the human body. These efforts at jazzing up the classroom routine were not always successful, such as the time Aghor Babu unwrapped a paper parcel and showed a shocked Rabi a portion of the human windpipe before he began to expound on the marvels of its mechanism. Aghor Babu's problem was not his person, but his subject, English, that over the years caused Rabi much grief and occasional merriment.

How well do I remember the day our tutor tried to impress on us the attractiveness of the English language. With this object he recited to us with sweet unction some lines—prose or poetry we could not tell—from an English book. It had a most unlooked-for effect on us. We laughed so immoderately that he had to dismiss us for that evening.[8]

And although later he became proficient in English—he translated *Macbeth* for his tutor when he was only twelve and one of his early volumes includes translations of many English poets such as Shelley, Christina Rossetti, Swinburne and Mrs Browning—Rabindranath was never to lose his early ambivalence towards the language. His argument for the mother tongue as the medium of a child's instruction remains as incisive today as it was then and needs to be widely disseminated when the demand for schooling in English, from the primary level onward, is being raised by parents in many parts of India.

It was because we were taught in our own language that our minds quickened. Learning should as far as possible follow the process of eating. When the taste begins from the first bite, the stomach is awakened to its function before it is loaded, so that its digestive juices get full play. Nothing like this happens, however, when a Bengali boy is taught in English. The first bite bids fair to wrench loose both rows of teeth—like an earthquake in the mouth! And by the time he discovers that the morsel is not of the genus stone, but a digestible bonbon, half his allotted span of life is over. While one is choking and spluttering over the spelling and grammar, the inside remains starved; and when at length the taste comes through, the appetite has vanished. If the whole mind is not functioning from the beginning, its full powers remain undeveloped to the end. While all around was the cry for English teaching, my third brother was brave enough to keep us to our Bengali course. To him in heaven my grateful reverence.[9]

As a poet, Rabindranath is alive to the danger of 'operational thinking', that is, verbal expressions lacking associational links with feelings, symbols and memories, if the early education has been in an alien language. One's mother tongue, the language of one's childhood, is intimately linked with emotionally coloured sensory-motor experiences and however grammatically correct and rich the vocabulary of its user, the alien language will suffer from an emotional poverty that is generally fatal to the enterprise of poetry.

Rabi's misery continued in all the schools he attended and his memories of the third school, Bengal Academy, which he entered when he was around twelve, are representative for the other three.

> What was taught there we never understood, neither did we make any attempt to learn, and it did not seem to make any difference to anybody that we did not. . .
>
> This school had one great advantage for me. No one there cherished the forlorn hope that boys of our sort could make any advance in learning. In a petty institution with an insufficient income, so that we had one supreme merit in the eyes of its authorities—we paid our fees regularly. . .
>
> Still, harmless though it was, after all it was a school. The rooms were cruelly dismal with their walls on guard like policemen. The house was more like a pigeon-holed box than a human habitation. No decoration, no pictures, not a touch of colour, not an attempt to attract the boyish heart. The fact that likes and dislikes form a large part of the child-mind was completely ignored. Naturally our whole being was depressed as we stepped through its doorway into the narrow quadrangle—and playing truant became chronic with us.[10]

Looking closely at his account of his school years, it seems to me that it is not only the monotony and the regimented nature of formal schooling or the lack of aesthetics in the school buildings and environment that made Rabi's rejection verge on a phobic school refusal. As the second site of identity development after the family, the responses a child gets from his interactions with his teachers and other children in school play a considerable role in his budding sense of identity, of who he is and will become. Identity is a two-step construction wherein my view of myself must be in the next step that is almost a simultaneous transaction confirmed by my significant group for its completion. Lacking outer confirmation, an aspired identity remains fragile. Self-definition without external validation has the same status as that of an inmate of a psychiatric facility who believes he is Jesus.

Because of the greater 'relational' cast of the Indian mind which I have described elsewhere,[11] a mind that dreads the fate of being an atom and consistently strives to be a molecule, the identity-giving power of a person's social group becomes even more crucial in the Indian setting than in other, more 'individualistic' societies. This is especially true of a child like Rabi who grew up in a large extended family, and who became highly sensitized to the moods and needs of others from a very early age. In addition to the high social sensitivity produced by the Indian cultural context, this stage of life which psychoanalysis calls the latency period, is also characterized by the universal need of the child to be accepted by his peers. Rabi was not only isolated and rejected by other boys but actively victimized and bullied; once while being chased by some older boys he ran crying for protection into the room of Gobinda Babu, the feared school superintendent.

> As my memories of the Normal School [the second school he attended] emerge from haziness and become clearer they are not the least sweet in any particular. Had I been able to associate with other boys, the woes of learning might not have seemed so intolerable. But that turned out to be impossible—so nasty were

most of the boys in their manners and habits. So, in the intervals
of the classes, I would go up to the second storey and while away
the time sitting near a window overlooking the street. I would
count: one year—two years—three years—; wondering how many
such I would have to get through like this.[12]

In the next school, Bengal Academy, his situation was not much
better.

The boys here were annoying but not disgusting—which was a
great comfort. They wrote 'ASS' on their palms and slapped it on to
our backs with a cordial 'hello!' They gave us a dig in the ribs from
behind and looked innocently another way. They dabbed banana
pulp on our heads and made away unperceived. Nevertheless it
was like coming out of slime on the rock—we were worried but
not soiled.[13]

It is not difficult to understand the bullying behaviour of Rabi's
schoolmates. He, as also the slightly older Satya and Soumendra,
were *the* Tagores, scions of the family of 'Prince' Dwarkanath
Tagore, Calcutta's leading businessman and India's first industrial
entrepreneur who had been received by Queen Victoria herself.
Known for his lavish lifestyle, Dwarkanath had not only been a
financial success but was also a philanthropist involved in founding
major institutions of national importance: the National Library,
the Agricultural and Horticultral Society of India, Calcutta Medical
College. And although the Tagores may have been financially
on a downward slide from the heyday of the 'Indian Croseus', as
Dwarkanath was called in Europe on his frequent travels abroad,
they were still one of the wealthier families of Bengal, with large
land holdings in the eastern part of the province. Widely regarded
as among the pioneers of the Indian Renaissance, the position

of the Tagore family at the forefront of Bengal's cultural life was unchallenged. It was also an unconventional family where many orthodox Hindu rituals and codes of conduct no longer found a welcoming home. The sense of uniqueness that came from the family's relative isolation from others—that is, from it having 'raised the social anchor and drifted away from conventional moorings'— extended to the characteristic style of the language of the family members which people of Calcutta called 'Tagore-speak'.[14] To the other boys, Rabi must have appeared a snooty 'nabob' who was driven to and back from school in a closed horse carriage and, worse, made no bones about wanting to avoid their company; in all of his school years, Rabi mentions only one school friend who he ever visited at his home or who was invited to Jorasanko.

Rabi's shyness that made him keep to himself at school must have appeared as arrogance, his delicate sensibility that abhorred coarseness as setting himself apart and above the other boys, a haughty if silent condemnation of their boisterous boorishness. Moreover, it must have been galling to the other boys that although he was an indifferent student, Rabi had one dubious gift—for writing poetry—which made him a favourite of the school superintendent who would openly hold up Rabi in front of the class as a model for the other boys to emulate. As one can imagine, this particular giftedness is not one that elicits a pre-teen boy's admiration. In fact, quite the opposite. Boys of this age—and this applies across cultures—admire other boys who are talented in what is considered 'phallic' and masculine behaviour: outdoor sports, undertakings involving manual dexterity and physical aggressiveness, activities in organized and unorganized male groups, including predatory gangs, certainly not the scribbling of verse. It is unsurprising that the other boys would seek retribution on a hapless Rabi through phallic aggressiveness characteristic of the latency years, manifested in sadistic bullying. Rabi's hatred for schools was then not only because of the monotony of their teaching methods and aesthetic deficiencies of their environment but also because of his daily humiliation and isolation from his peers in not being a 'boy's boy'.

Latency years are not only crucial for the development of a boy's self-image of his intellectual capacity and potential, his ability to master the skills and tasks required by the school, and his view of his own social competence and efficacy in the world outside the family, but also for finding and strengthening his masculine identity. Rabi's break with the maternal-feminine world of infancy and early childhood might have been abrupt but it would take the years of the latency period before a psychological emancipation from the feminine within—never complete nor even completely desired, or desirable—could take place. In a chapter titled 'The Professor' in his *Reminiscences*, his title for the older boy mentioned earlier with whom he had struck a friendship, Rabindranath reveals his masculine vulnerability which, paradoxically, as we shall see later, also became a strength for the creative work of his adult years. But to come back to the incident which Rabindranath deems 'worth a digression'.[15]

Rabi was eleven years old at the time, at the beginning of puberty, a boy with a slender frame that belied its suppleness and strength gained from daily gymnastic and wrestling lessons. He was shy, delicate of feature and with large, soulful eyes. Rabi greatly admired this older boy who was an 'expert in magic' and had even written a booklet on the subject—hence his title 'The Professor'. The boy used to take a lift back from school in the Tagore carriage till one day Rabi noticed that he would not sit on the same side as him and became self-conscious in Rabi's proximity. One day, the 'Professor-boy' asked the other boys to jump in turn from the schoolroom bench. He became thoughtful after Rabi, too, had jumped. Another day he asked the Tagore boys to his home where some of his other friends were waiting. They expressed an eagerness to hear Rabi sing.

I sang a song or two. Mere child as I was I could hardly have bellowed like a bull. 'Quite a sweet voice,' they all agreed.

When refreshments were put before us they sat round and watched us eat. I was bashful by nature and not used to strange company; moreover the habit I acquired during the attendance of our servant Ishwar had left me a poor eater for good. They all seemed impressed with the delicacy of my appetite.[16]

Rabi now started receiving what he calls 'some curiously warm letters' from the 'Professor'. What had happened was that Satya had told the boy that Rabi was actually a girl disguised as a boy so that she could have access to better schooling. Rabi's appearance and effeminate behaviour—he had even jumped like 'a girl is supposed to jump with her left foot forward'—had convinced the older boy of the truth of Satya's mischievous claim. What a reader may find odd is that Rabindranath is not more surprised that a friend of long-standing with whom he shared many rides in the carriage on the way back from school could actually believe that Rabi was a girl.

As in the early years of servocracy, Rabi's imagination again tried to fight off the feelings of helplessness and humiliation; while other boys recited their lessons, young Rabi sat silently at the back of the class, fantasizing about training an army of ferocious dogs, tigers and other wild beasts to send to the battlefield and '. . .defeat an enemy without having arms.'[17] On his return from school, he would seek to reconnect with the two revitalizing sites of his solitude: the inner garden and the roof terrace. It was the sight of the coconut trees in the inner garden, he says, each one with 'a distinct personality' and, looking up at and beyond the terrace to the 'blue-grey water-laden clouds thickly banked up' in the sky that filled him with an 'immense depth of gladness'.[18] Unlike most children, Rabi stubbornly refused to give up the subjective inner reality of his fantasy life and accept the objective reality of the outer world—a step essential for normal development but fatal for a would-be poet or artist.

What saved the boy Rabi from developing an enduring sense of inadequacy and inferiority, both with regard to his intellectual capability and social desirability, was a counteracting stream of messages from a few men in his environment that he was special in a way other boys were not. The specialness lay in the fact that at the age of eight Rabi got hold of a blue-paper manuscript book, made irregular pencil lines in it and began to write verses in a large scrawl.[19] The preening pleasure which Rabi felt on being recognized as a 'poet' comes through clearly in Rabindranath's modest and ironic account of his first steps into poetry.

His first admirer was his eldest brother Dwijendranath, himself an aspiring poet, who would buttonhole visitors to the house, especially those connected with literary life, and ask Rabi to recite one or the other of his poems. Even in the awful schools there was a teacher, Satkari Babu, who would send for the boy and ask him to complete a quatrain by adding a couplet to the one given by him. And then there was the dreaded Gobinda Babu, the superintendent of the school, who called Rabi to his office one day and asked him to write a poem on a moral precept. The next day, when Rabi handed him the verses, Gobinda Babu took Rabi to the highest class and, standing before the older boys, asked him to recite the poem which Rabi did, loudly.

Rabi's greatest admirer, one for whom Rabindranath has the fondest sentiments was Srikantha Babu, 'a hearer the like of whom I shall never get again'.[20] A true innocent, without a trace of malice or coarseness in his nature, Srikantha Babu, who taught Rabi to sing, was equally at home in the company of the boys as he was with the men of the Tagore household. Full of enthusiasm for Rabi's poetic productions he would try to acquaint the adults— once even reaching the otherwise inaccessible father—with his favourite pupil's poetic prowess. In the pride Rabi felt in his first poetic creations, one can sense the dawning of a still inchoate realization that he may be part of a small tribe of the elect, the makers of culture, not the large horde of its consumers.

Rabi grasped at the identity of the poet that was offered him with all the strength of his slender arms. Like the scaffolding that holds up a crumbling building, the poet-identity was indispensable in shoring up a depleted and shaky sense of self-esteem although the feeling of being 'worthless' and 'unlovable' never completely disappeared. In March 1893, writing to his niece Indira, with whom he could be quite honest, Rabindranath says:

Often I think that had it not been for my poetic strength or a few other natural talents, then there would be only a few like me in this world, so unbearable, fruitless. Even I am born worthless, but due to my capacity to write I have somehow managed to get away with it in this life-time. Otherwise none of you would have been able to love me at all. That I know for sure. The fact that everyone loves 'Suri' [his nephew] is not because of his work, or power, or any effort—but rather due to his inner integrity and beauty. . .Being born in this world I have got you all as my relatives and I remain forever grateful for that. Only I know how much all of you have helped me. Those who are good human beings would not know what value their love has. That you and Suri love me, still amazes me though I may even somewhat expect it. If I think deep enough, I feel that I do not deserve anything that is good at all, everything has been granted with special permission—I have received so much and so easily that I may not often understand how unbelievably bountiful they are, if ever there is even a little bit that is amiss, it feels like an unfair rejection! Man's ungratefulness is the greatest sign of his undeserving nature.[21]

In the next few years, Rabi assiduously cultivated the poet-identity. For instance, while travelling with his father at the age of twelve to Bolpur, he tells us that, ignoring the burning heat of the day and the hard, unturfed gravel, he wrote poetry: 'I loved to do it sprawling under a young coconut palm. This seemed to me the true manner'[22] since 'It was not just writing poems, but holding a picture of myself as a poet before my imagination' that was important to him.[23]

It was this identity of a poet that he would cling to in his darker hours throughout his life: 'I was born a poet...I am not an athlete, I do not belong to an arena; the stare of the curious crowd scorches my soul. . .',[24] 'Why should I be anything else but a poet? Was I not born a music maker?'[25] he would sometimes plaintively state and at others proudly assert.

Rabindranath remained highly ambivalent towards all the other identities that were ascribed and offered to him in his adult years: philosopher, educationist, man of letters, the wise man from the East, Gandhi's 'The Great Sentinel', and so on. To his friend C.F. Andrews he would mock his different personas, refusing to acknowledge that they constituted and could ever compete with his fundamental identity as a poet.

> And am I not a poet? What business have I to try and be anything else? But unfortunately I am like an inn where the poet lodger has to accommodate strange bed-fellows by his side. But is it not high time for me to retire from this none too lucrative business of innkeeper? Anyhow I am feeling tired and my duty to my numerous lodgers is imminently in danger of being shamefully neglected.[26]

And at another place, after talking of the Poet within:

> Sometimes it amuses me to observe the struggle for supremacy that is going on between the different persons within me: Practical

Man, Patriotic Man, Man who is Good. As for me, who am the president of this Panchayat, I have my deepest sentiment of tenderness for this Poet, possibly because he is utterly good for nothing and who is first to be ignored in the time of emergency...I simply jump up from my judgment seat and holding the Poet by the hand dance a jig and sing:

> I shall join you, comrade,
> and be drunk, and be gloriously useless.

Ah, my evil luck! I know why Presidents of meetings hate me, newspaper editors revile me, the virile call me effeminate and I try to take my shelter among children who have the gift of being glad with things and men that have no value.[27]

The poet was the child within, not the melancholic child of exile and loneliness but the child of solitude and soaring imagination, transforming the hurts and defeats of the former into triumphs. On board the ship bound for India, he writes to Andrews:

Dear friend, the very fact that we have turned our face towards the east fills my heart with joy. For me my east is the poet's east, not that of a politician or a scholar. It is the east of the magnanimous sky and exuberant sunlight where once upon a time a boy found himself straying in the dim twilight of child-consciousness peopled with dreams. That child has grown, but never grown out of his child-ness. I realize it all the more strongly when some problem, political or otherwise, becomes clamorous and insistent, trying to exact its answer from me. I rouse myself up, I strain my mind, I raise my voice for prophetic utterances, in every way try to be worthy of the occasion, but in my heart of heart I feel exceedingly small and to my utter dismay I discover I am not a leader, not a speaker, not a teacher and furthest away from being a prophet. The fact becomes fully evident to me that I had forgotten to grow.[28]

Even while thoroughly involved in his cherished project of setting up an international university in Shantiniketan that would combine the best of East and West, for which he had to travel often to Europe and the USA in search for financial, moral and intellectual support, Rabindranath would bemoan the deathly injury he was inflicting on the poet within by following a dream that was not part of his core identity.

> While my companion was this eternal Piper, this Spirit of Play, I was nearest to the heart of the world, I knew its mother tongue, and what I sang was caught up by the chorus of the wind and water and the dance-master of life. But how came the schoolmaster in the midst of my dream world and I was foolish enough to accept his guidance? I laid aside my reed, I left my playground where the Infinite Child is spending his eternity 'in mere idle sport'. In a moment I became old and carried the burden of wisdom on my back, hawking truths from door to door...Pushing the wheelbarrow of propaganda from continent to continent, is this going to be the climax of a poet's life?. . .You know I have said somewhere that 'God praises me when I do good but God loves me when I sing.'[29]

On these European and American tours in the 1920s, Rabindranath's reputation was at its height. Wherever he went, he was lionized by huge crowds that turned up for his talks, people pressing around him to touch the hem of his robe, even kiss it in reverence. Amidst all the narcissistic gratification that such an enthusiastic reception brought him, Rabindranath was keenly aware that fame was an acute danger to his poet-identity, that success could undermine his own 'truth'. Writing to Andrews from Europe, Rabindranath describes his dilemma:

It is far better for a poet to miss his reward in this life than to have a false reward or to have it in excessive measure. The man who constantly received honour from admiring crowds has the grave danger of developing a habit of mental parasitism upon such honour—he consciously or unconsciously grows to crave for it and feels injured when his allowance is curtailed or withdrawn. I feel frightened of such possibility in me—for it is vulgar. Unfortunately when a person has some mission of doing some kind of public good, his popularity becomes the best asset for him—his own people readily follow him when other people have the same readiness—and this makes it a matter of temptation for such an individual. My International University is sure to create such a risk for me. And yet fulfillment of my life is never in any ambitious scheme like this. And therefore a voice of warning is constantly troubling me in my heart, it cries: 'Poet, fly away to your solitude.'[30]

As he aged and the favours of his Muse became fitful and increasingly capricious, Rabindranath would cry out:

One day I shall have to fight my way out of my own reputation— for the call of my Padma still comes to me through this huge and growing barrier. It says—'Poet, where are you?' and all my heart and soul try to seek out that poet. It has been difficult to find him—for the great multitude of men have heaped honours on him—and he cannot be extricated from under them.[31]

To remind himself he was a poet, to reconnect to the only stream of admiration that was available to him in childhood and to unconsciously conjure up the glow in the eyes of his elder brother, Srikantha Babu and perhaps some other adults whose names we no longer know—anonymous helpers in the realization of his destiny—was not only a bulwark against intimations of identity disintegration, but also a means to revive the memories of utter well being in finding a home in poetry, a focus for his special kind of imagination. Imagination was no longer diffuse 'fancy' but, yoked to the discipline of poetic form, became the driving force in his creativity. Perhaps it is the smooth working partnership between imagination and discipline, a playful combination of the two, that goes into the making of a poet or indeed animates any creative enterprise. Imagination, the dream, provides the inspiration for the creative impulse; disciplined knowledge, the craft, the execution. But we must not forget that while the creative impulse may be conceived in the unconscious of the artist or poet, it needs human midwives to give it expression in the outer world. We need to remember our debts to the humble midwives—Dwijendranath, Srikantha Babu but also the teacher Satkari Babu, the school superintendent Gobinda Babu—for assisting in the birth of the poet Rabindranath.

6

The Way of the Father

In many ways, Rabi's father, Debendranath, was as remarkable a person as his grandfather Dwarkanath. Whereas Dwarkanath was known as the 'Prince', not because of his aristocratic origins but because of his lavish spending and opulent lifestyle, Debendranath came to be called the Maharishi, an appellation given to ancient Indian sages, saintly mystics living a life of renunciation.

This was not always so. As a youth, Debendranath had led the pleasure-loving life of a young man from a wealthy family. Then, at the age of eighteen, on the eve of his beloved grandmother's death, a spiritual transformation took place. While growing up, Didima, the grandmother, had been the person Debendranath had been closest to. As he recalls in the first sentences of his autobiography, 'My grandmother was very fond of me. To me, also, she was all in all during the days of my childhood. My sleeping, sitting, eating, all were at her side.'[1]

When Didima took mortally ill and according to custom was taken to the bank of the Ganges to die, Debendranath was with her the three days and nights before she passed away. On the night before she died, a night of full moon, Debendranath was sitting on a coarse mat near the shed on the riverbank in which his grandmother was lying, listening to the deathbed chanting by the priests.

> The sounds reached my ears faintly, borne on the night wind; at this opportune moment a strange sense of the unreality of all things suddenly entered my mind. I was no longer the same man. A strong aversion to wealth arose within me. The coarse bamboo-mat on which I sat seemed to be my fitting seat, carpets and costly spreadings seemed hateful, in my mind was awakened a joy unfelt before. . .With this sense of joy and renunciation, I returned home at midnight. That night I could not sleep. It was this blissful state of mind that kept me awake. Throughout the night my heart was suffused with a moonlight radiance of joy. At daybreak I went again to the riverside to see Didima. She was then drawing her last breaths.[2]

Both in the West and East, there are many such reported instances of spontaneous mystical experience following a cataclysmic psychic event that shocks the individual's body-mind entity out of its habitual way of being in the world. Very often, this event is the loss of a deeply beloved person, and it frequently happens in youth. Mystical illumination, though, may not be reduced to a defensive or compensatory phenomenon occasioned by the loss, the former caused by the latter. All one can say is that in certain exceptional individuals, the traumatic grief that overwhelms the mind's normal defences also makes it permeable to a mysterious energy, a 'divine' force, that leads to an intense heightening of consciousness. In the melancholy that returns after the mystical experience has ended, the individual mourns the loss of its all too brief exaltation. The mystical vision changes the course of mourning, gives grief another focus; the melancholy at the loss of the loved one is transformed into the mystic's 'dark night of the soul'.

In the days that followed, Debendranath's state of mind 'was one of continued despondency and indifference to the world.'

> On that night the indifference had been coupled with delight. Now,
> in the absence of that delight, a deep gloom settled on my mind.
> I longed for a repetition of that ecstatic feeling. I lost interest in
> everything else.[3]

This state of mind continued for some years, a state where 'The
temptations of the world had ceased, but the sense of God was no
nearer; earthly and heavenly happiness were alike withdrawn. Life
was dreary, the world was like a graveyard. I found happiness in
nothing; peace in nothing.'[4]

Like many others who have travelled on the mystical path,
Debendranath sought answers, and solace, in religious and spiritual
texts. He finally found his vocation in the leadership of the Brahmo
Samaj, a reformist Hindu movement started by Rammohan Roy that
sought a return to the 'pure' religion of the Upanishads and strongly
disapproved of Hinduism's rituals and idolatory.

Debendranath's ambition was as lofty as his ideals:

> All our theologians revere the Upanishads as the Vedanta, the
> crowning point and essence of all the Vedas. If I could preach
> Brama Dharma as based upon the Vedanta, then all India would
> have one religion, all dissensions would come to an end, all would
> be united in common brotherhood, her former valour and power
> would be revived, and finally she would regain her freedom.[5]

Debendranath was twenty-five when he took over the reins of
the Brahmo Samaj, an institution that had been in the doldrums
since Rammohan Roy's death nine years earlier. Debendranath
rejuvenated the Samaj through many new activities: publishing a
journal on spiritual matters, selecting hymns and composing prayers

for the new 'religion', selecting priests and getting them trained in the recitation of the Vedas, setting up a printing press for the dissemination of Rammohan Roy's writings, winning converts for the new movement, taking the lead in setting up a Hindu school to compete with Christian missionary schools and thus, as he believed, stem the tide of conversion to Christianity.

It is not surprising that Debendranath's chosen course of life would bring him in conflict with his worldly father, the creator of the Tagore family's wealth that consisted of large landholdings in north and east Bengal, extensive interests in indigo factories, saltpetre, sugar, tea and coal mines. As in most Indian families, the conflict between father and son was not overt. Simmering under the surface of traditional expressions of filial respect and being a dutiful son, Debendranath's 'rebellion' against his father, like that of many other Indian sons, was of a passive-aggressive kind where all the outer forms of politeness and deference were adhered to and would never progress to an open confrontation. Dwarakanath wanted his eldest son to follow his example and reach even greater heights of worldly success and was 'greatly grieved and despondent on finding the very reverse of this to be on my mind'.[6] Dwarkanath's love for the good things of life and throwing grand parties, especially for the British overlords, which excited snide comments in Calcutta society—'He only cares to take his pleasure with Englishmen, he never invites Bengalis'[7]—was countered by the son with his abstemious lifestyle and nationalist leanings. At an all-important garden party his father threw to appease Bengali society where the son was supposed to receive and entertain the guests, Debendranath was engrossed in his religious pursuits the whole day and much to his father's chagrin put in a hurried appearance before disappearing again.

Dwarkanath was also aware that during his absence on his first trip to England in 1841, Debendranath had completely neglected the running of the business, which he had left to subordinates, while he concerned himself with the Vedas, Vedanta, God and the ultimate goal of life. Prudently realizing that mystics do not make good businessmen or even managers, Dwarkanath placed four large estates in a family trust for the benefit of his three sons and their families to provide them a measure of security in case the family firm Carr, Tagore and Company, that took care of the business interests, ever landed in financial difficulty.

Within a year of his death, what Dwarkanath had feared came to pass; the firm went bankrupt, not in the least also because of the huge debts Dwarkanath himself had incurred in supporting his 'princely' lifestyle. The creditors took over the firm's assets and the family estates, settling an annual maintenance allowance of 25000 rupees on the Tagore family till the debts were cleared.

Debendranath writes of his happiness at this turn of events, which now allowed him to fully concentrate on his spiritual journey. He does not mention the anxiety that must have gripped his more worldly brothers and the women of the Tagore household at this sudden dip in their fortunes and the financial uncertainty brought in its wake.

> At this time I used to remain absorbed in thought upon deep philosophic doctrines from morning till noon. From noon till evening I would be engaged in studying the Vedas, the Vedanta, the Mahabharata, and such-like *shastras*, and in translating the Rigveda into Bengali. In the evening I used to sit on the terrace on a broad blanket. There Brahmos, seekers after Brahmo, and earnest seekers after the truth would come and sit by me and discuss various *shastras*. These discussions were sometimes carried on till after midnight.[8]

Even when, after a couple of years, the creditors returned the management of the estates to the three brothers, Debendranath

ceded the control in running of the firm to his younger brother
Girindranath so that he could remain free for his work in the Brahmo
Samaj and concentrate on his spiritual development.

Five years before Rabi's birth, Debendranath decided to leave
home. In the time-honoured Hindu tradition of renouncing the
world, he planned to lead the life of a wandering ascetic, a sannyasi,
though to ease the transition from a life of comfort to one of physical
hardship he prudently took his personal servant, Kishori, along
with him. He was away for two years. Much of this time was in the
Himalayas, during the period of the 1857 uprising against British
rule, when all of northern India was in an unsettled state. One day
in Shimla, as he sat on a rock, musing on the course of a stream
rushing down the hillside, gathering loose soil on the way, he heard
a Divine command:

> 'Give up thy pride, and be lowly like this river. The truth thou hast
> gained, the devotion and trustfulness that thou hast learnt here;
> go make them known to the world.'[9]

Obeying the voice of 'the Guide within me', Debendranath returned
to Calcutta, to resume his missionary work for the Brahmo Samaj. All
through the time Rabi was growing up, Debendranath would often
disappear into the Himalayas for long stretches of time, especially
during Durga Puja, to protest the 'idolatry' associated with this most
important and loved of Bengali festivals.

Debendranath, then, was like a remote and benevolent god,
without a palpable presence in family life, yet a fount of mystery
and awe to his children. I can imagine the eleven-year-old Rabi's
excitement and conflicting emotions of pride and apprehension at
perhaps not measuring up to this god-like figure's exacting standards
when, after his sacred thread ceremony that signalled his attaining
full Brahminhood had been performed, the father singled him out

to accompany him on a journey to the Himalayas.

The few months Rabi was away with his father left a deep impression on his psyche. The importance of these months may be gauged from the way that more than thirty-five years later, in his autobiography, Rabindranath can recollect the minutest details of the days he spent with his father. Rabi left Calcutta as a timid boy, tremulously taking his first steps into the outside world, terrified of his first train journey yet also exulting at his freedom from the rule of the servants. He returned as a confident youth, shy but no longer timorous, with clear-cut intimations of his future identity as a poet and as a man.

At first, the experience of freedom was exhilarating but had a touch of unreality, as if the sights he was gulping in with his eyes could vanish at any moment. On the first evening of their trip, when father and son arrived at Bolpur and climbed into the palanquin, Rabi kept his eyes closed so as to preserve the vision for the morning light and not have the freshness of his experience spoilt by incomplete glimpses caught in the twilight. As they went up the Himalayas in a jhampan, his 'eyes had no rest the whole day, so great was my fear lest anything should escape them'.[10]

Wherever they were, Debendranath did not place restrictions on Rabi's striking out on his own and exploring their surroundings. On the contrary, he encouraged his son's explorations of the valleys and plateaus around the house in which they settled in the hills. When Rabi discovered a hollow full of spring water in a ravine and excitedly asked whether they couldn't get their bathing and drinking water from there, the father shared his rapture and immediately ordered the servants to draw the water from that spring.

Although expecting the same standards of conduct from the boy as he did from everyone else—standards in which timings were to be strictly kept, promised tasks had to be performed without any laxity or slovenliness—Debendranath also treated Rabi as a

responsible adult. He put the boy in charge of the cash box from
which money was taken out for travel expenses. He entrusted him
with the task of daily winding his valuable gold watch. He marked
his favourite verses from the *Gita* and asked Rabi to copy out these
for him. 'At home I had been a boy of no account, but here, when
these important functions were entrusted to me, I fully felt the glory
of the situation.'[11]

Rabi's gratefulness and joy at the closeness he experiences with
his father for the first time in his life is palpable: Debendranth would
wake Rabi before dawn, the hour for the son to memorize his Sanskrit
declensions. As the sun appeared over the horizon and dawn broke,
father and son would stand together while the father communed
with the Divine, the Great Spirit, by chanting the Upanishads. They
would then go for an early morning walk in the hills. Rabi would
have his lessons during the day and wander on his own in the thickly
wooded forest of deodars below the house in the afternoons. In the
evenings, father and son would sit outside, gazing up at the sky with
its profusion of stars shining radiantly through the clear mountain
air, while Debendranath pointed out constellations or gave the boy
an impromptu astronomy lesson. Other evenings, Rabi would be
asked to sing:

> The moon has risen; its beams, passing through the trees, have
> fallen on the verandah floor; I am singing in the *Behaga* mode:
> > *O Companion in the darkest passage of life. . .*
> My father with bowed head and clasped hands is intently listening.
> I can recall this evening scene even now.[12]

Perhaps what is most important in the closeness Rabi shared with
his father during these few months is the fact that Debendranath
is no longer a mysterious, god-like figure evoking awe in the son.
Rather, he emerges as a man and father who offers his son the

opportunity for vital identifications that a boy needs in this period of his life if he is to develop a secure identity as a man and a particular kind of 'worker'. In other words, Debendranath became a viable and meaningful parent precisely at the time the pre-adolescent boy urgently needed one, even if it was only for a few months. The shift from paternal awe to paternal respect is evident in Rabindranath's descriptions of the father such as:

> As he allowed me to wander about the mountains at my will, so in the quest for truth he left me to free to select my path. He was not deterred by the danger of my making mistakes, he was not alarmed at the prospect of my encountering sorrow. He held up a standard, not a disciplinary rod.[13]

Written a couple of years after his father's death, Rabindranath perhaps exaggerates the father's relinquishing of control on his son's life. As we shall see later, although Debendranath was tolerant of Rabi's vocation as a poet, contributing to his flowering as one, this tolerance did not extend to other areas of life, such as family obligations regarding marriage or management of the family estates. Artistic creativity is certainly possible in opposition to the father but it will be one that is fraught with recurrent emotional conflict.

Debendranath's possession of such qualities that the son could respect and admire, and Rabi's strong need of building a male identity converged in an idealization of the father that was lifelong, and one that made an identification with the father possible.

Identification, which involves the unconscious fantasy of becoming like the other person, focuses on the model's selected qualities and here, Debendranath offered his youngest son his high ethical standards and an independence of spirit that encourages a disregard of social convention and opinions of others to follow a star that lights one's own path alone. There were other identifications, too.

The Maharshi's indifference to human ties, perhaps even a coldness, in contrast to the passion generated in his soul by the transcendent, also finds an echo in his son's psyche. Debendranath's passionate hatred of idolatory—which was so strong that he was willing to antagonize the extended Tagore family and all their friends by refusing to follow traditional, 'idolatrous' ceremonies at 'Prince' Dwarkanath's funeral—reverberate in his son's uncharacteristic outburst:

> I'd like to sweep up every idol of every kind, brass, wood, stone and alabaster, from every city and village—every temple and mahulla, and make one great heap from the whole country, and sweep them into the sea and so cleanse our stables.[14]

Most important, though, the father also gave Rabi access to the core of his identity—his spirituality. No longer catching a glimpse of the meditating father from afar, as in Jorasanko, but being witness to the Maharshi's absorption in the Divine from the closest quarters, praying together in the mornings as the sun rises above the mountain peaks, Rabi's identification with his father's spiritual concerns would, so to speak, give him sanction to reinforce and consolidate the spiritual aspect of his own identity.

Rabi's idealization submerged but did not eradicate every negative feeling, such as that of an unconscious rivalry—hinted at in a couple of poems in *The Crescent Moon*—a boy may also have towards his father. For instance, at the age of seventeen, in England and thus at a 'safe' distance away from the family and at the beginning of youth, a period where early childhood conflicts are again revived, Rabi gives vent to his resentment at the aloof and emotionally distant father and the absolute authority he (and the father-like elder brothers) wielded over his life, together with chagrin and self-reproach at his own meek, weak-kneed submission to this authority. In a long letter to his sister-in-law, he complains of the abnormal respect and unnatural fear commanded by elders in the family.

> During childhood, it is constantly chanted into our ears that our
> father and other elders are like God. Why? Why should they be
> like God? Why should the stern and distant reverence of godliness
> be inflicted upon them? They are our beloved fathers and mothers;
> we should be united with them in the free embrace of love, and
> not humbly with folded hands.[15]

Veiled by what are purported to be general observations on fathers
and sons in the Indian setting, Rabi's own protest in relation to
Debendranath is not difficult to discern.

> Should we go, instead of to our human fathers, to a godlike
> person, leading an ascetic life outside our society and sit by
> him with utmost hesitation, and, talking softly, offer ourselves
> humbly? Which of these two possibilities is natural? We heap
> unnatural reverence upon the elders of our families, and they
> in turn, empowered by our blind faith, behave with the younger
> ones in any way they please. They want their children to accept
> unquestioningly, without the least objection or hesitation, their
> every command and judgment, as though they were wooden
> clockwork toys without minds, without mentalities, without
> desires, without the faculty of judgment.[16]

It must have been a source of anguish to young Rabindranath that
when it came to the crunch—his marriage, to which I'll come back
later—he could only cross his father in his imagination, never in
action.

In his relationship with his father, we see the presence of yet
another duality in Rabindranath's psyche: grandfather–father, the
former worldly and sensual, the other determinedly spiritual and
filled with the spirit of renunciation. On one side is Dwarkanath:

cosmopolitan and, like Rabindranath, at ease with, and in fact preferring, the social life of England and Europe, so much so that people called him an 'English lover'. He is the un-person who is absent in Rabindranath's autobiographies, but nevertheless exercises an unconscious fascination in indicating to the grandson the attraction of a wider, cosmopolitan identity, beyond the confines of a narrow Indianness. Rabindranath would, like his grandfather, appreciate the vigour and dash of Western civilization, though unlike the latter he would not fully embrace it. On the other side, as we saw, is the consciously idealized Debendranath: ascetic, staunchly Indian, his goal in life the restoration of the glory of ancient Hindu civilization through the reformist Brahmo Samaj.

After five months, the father–son idyll came to an end. While Debendranath stayed back in the mountain retreat, Rabi returned to Calcutta, 'brimming with health and spirits'. His homecoming was a triumphant affair.

> The chains of the rigorous regime which had bound me snapped for good when I had set out from home. . .When I arrived it was not merely a homecoming from travel, it was also a return from my exile in the servants' quarters to my proper place in the inner apartments. Whenever the inner household assembled in my mother's room I now occupied a seat of honour.[17]

The next chapter in our youthful hero's story—momentous in the shaping his psyche and one whose reverberations continued to haunt Rabindranath for the rest of his life—was thus heralded by the exuberant flourishes of a twelve-year-old boy on the cusp of youth. I am, of course, speaking of the love of his life, the earthly Muse for so much of his creative work, a young girl, merely two years older than Rabi, who had entered the Tagore family four years earlier as the child-bride of his twelve-years-older brother, Jyotirindranath.

7

Kadambari, and the Smell of
Buttered Toast

Rabi's seven years of exile from the *andar mahal*, the inner quarters of the Tagore women, did not come to an end just because the travel with his father had somehow conferred on him a new status. The journey to the Himalayas was not a reverse initiation rite that allowed Rabi entry into the world of women. The *andar mahal* and the terrace became accessible simply because the brooding presence of the high-minded father, a presence that was inhibiting even when the patriarch was away, was suddenly lifted. This is apparent from the casual first lines of the chapter in *Boyhood Days* that seek to recapture memories of a period Rabindranath would consider as the happiest of his life, one in which he had felt most alive:

A fresh breeze was blowing in the kingdom of the terrace, a new season had arrived. Our esteemed father had left the Jorasanko House, by then. Jyotida took up residence in the room on the second floor. In the corner of that room, I carved a tiny niche for myself.[1]

The main actor for years in the inner theatre of Rabi's adolescence and early youth—playing a crucial role both in the remembered

107

happiness of those years and the consolidation of his identity as a poet and writer—was his sister-in-law, Kadambari Devi.

Rabindranath's first memory-picture of Kadambari is that of a ten-year-old girl with 'thin gold bangles on her tender dark wrists' whom he 'circled from afar, afraid to come close'.[2] She had entered the Tagore household as Jyotirindranath's bride, and as far as Rabi was concerned this sister-in-law, barely two years older than him, had right away disappeared into the fastness of the women's quarters. She now emerged, four years later, to declare 'the advent of a new dispensation' which Rabindranath compares to rainfloods descending from far-off hills, undermining the foundations of ancient dams.[3] Rabi's long pent-up feelings of affection, warmth, love—of Eros in all its multi-hued splendour— gushed out, in song as much as in the subterranean regions of the psyche we blithely call the 'heart' which, in Rabi's case, 'like the breed of grasshopper that blends its hue with the colour of dry leaves', had for so many years worn 'a faded tint, to merge with the dryness' of his days.[4]

Kadambari, a practically illiterate girl for whom books on elementary arithmetic and Bengali had to be purchased when she first became part of the Tagore family, was a remarkable young woman who grew up to be at the centre of Jorasanko's literary activities, and Muse to the boy destined to be the most famous Tagore of all. An incurable romantic, she was yet energetic and bold. Taught horseback riding by a liberal husband, she daily rode out to the Maidan, causing a furore in traditional Bengali society where such a pastime was the province of the British memsahibs and the odd Indian woman who aspired to be a 'brown mem'.

Kadambari's family was undistinguished, far below that of the Tagores in economic and social standing, not to speak of artistic and literary accomplishment. Her grandfather had been employed by Rabi's grandfather Dwarkanath as a taster whose job was to taste the freshness of sandesh, Bengal's signature sweet, that was supplied to the household every day.[5] The only argument in favour of the match, one that proved to be critical in a highly caste conscious society, was that Kadambari's family was of the same caste as the Tagores: Pirali Brahmins. These were Brahmins who were considered unmarriageable by the orthodox after two of their ancestors in the fifteenth century had unwittingly tasted beef at the court of Mohammmed Pir Ali, the minister of the governor of Jessore. The two brothers were thrown out of Hindu society and had then converted to Islam. Down through the centuries, their relatives, who remained Hindu, were still considered to be polluted. Even in the nineteenth century, the persistent ostracism of Pirali Brahmins was so strong that when in 1852 an orthodox Brahmin boy married Rabindranath's cousin, he was expelled from his family.[6] For all his reformist zeal, Debendranath was unwilling to challenge this particular taboo on marrying outside caste, and thus the choice of mates for the men and women of the Tagore family was severely limited.

If Kadambari played the lead, then her husband Jyotirindranath was indispensable as supporting cast in the transformation of a diffident and often unhappy boy into a carefree youngster, increasingly confident of his poetic powers and sanguine about the destiny that awaited him. The pleasure-loving Jyotirindranath, his easy-going ways a complete contrast to those of the grave father, was not only fond of music, dance and theatre but himself spent most of his mornings writing plays or composing catchy tunes on the piano. He encouraged Rabi, who had finally dropped out of his fourth (and last) school after another year of misery, to sit beside him while he played. Rabi's task—if it can be called one for a boy aspiring to be a poet—was to provide the lyrics to the melodies.

In the afternoons, while Jyotirindranath was away in the office for a few hours of desultory work connected with the management of family estates, Rabi would read out loud to Kadambari who preferred to receive the gifts of literature through her ears than her eyes. The readings would be his own poems or writings of Bengali literary icons of the time, such as Bankim Chandra's novel *Bishabriksha* (The Poison Tree) that was being serialized in a popular journal, *Bangadarshan*, at the time. The image of those sultry afternoons—the boy declaiming his verse to an intent young woman who is fanning him with a hand-held fan to stir a faint cooling breeze—is one of the most memorable scenes in Satyajit Ray's film *Charulata*, based on Rabindranath's own fictional representation of those halcyon days. In dedicating his poems—composed between the ages of thirteen and eighteen , and collected in 'Shoishabsangeet' (Childhood Songs)—to Kadambari, Rabindranath says that he wrote them sitting next to her, reading them to her, and all the memories of those affectionate moments are alive in these poems.[7]

Kadambari was not only Rabi's intimate companion in his journey as a budding poet, but also caretaker of his more prosaic, corporeal needs. For a boy like Rabi, who had become resigned to the frugal and tasteless meals dished out by the servants, Kadambari's lovingly cooked dishes that replaced his earlier ruder fare were a gustatory revelation, as much a sign of her love as the serious attention with which she listened to his songs. Ailing and close to death, Rabindranath could still summon the taste of his favourite, mashed *chorchori*, mixed vegetables prepared with shrimp with a light flavouring of chillies, which Kadambari cooked specially for him.

In the evenings, Rabi joined Jyotirindranath and Kadambari on the terrace that had been transformed by her into a garden with rows of tall palms along the balustrades, surrounded by sweet-smelling flowering shrubs—oleander, tuberose, chameli, champa. At the age of eighty, Rabindranath's boyhood memories of those enchanted evenings are as sensual as they are precise.

> At the end of the day, mats and bolsters would be arranged on
> the terrace. On a silver dish, jasmine garlands wrapped in damp

handkerchiefs would be placed, there would be a tumbler of iced
water on a saucer, and in a bowl, fragrant paan of the indigenous
variety. Freshly bathed and dressed, her hair coiffed, Bouthakrun
[Kadambari] would take her place. Jyotidada would appear, a light
wrap cast airily across his shoulders. He would put his bow to the
violin, and I would launch into a song on a high note. The Creator
has never taken away the slight talent for music he had granted
me. Across the rooftop my song would carry, and into the sunset
sky. From the far-off sea, the southern breeze would blow, and
the sky would fill with stars.[8]

Like the children which the two adolescents also were, Rabi and
Kadambari would sometimes bicker. It is unjust to keep squirrels
in a cage, he would tell her. Stop acting like a schoolmaster, she
would retort. Further remonstrances would follow after Rabi
had surreptitiously released the two caged squirrels. Kadambari's
fondness for fashionable clothes was occasion for repeated quarrels.
Rabi wanted her to wear old-fashioned white, black-bordered
saris rather than the fashionable dresses of silk and lace which she
preferred. Rabi would express his distaste for such superficiality; she
was better than that, after all.

How deeply it upset me, I cannot describe. I would repeatedly
object, in great agitation. Act your age: no need to behave as if
you're my uncle!—would be her reply. . .I could never win a debate
with Bouthakrun, because she never countered my arguments. I
also lost to her at chess, at which she was an expert.[9]

From Rabindranath's fond memories of their wrangling, such
as the times when she was away visiting relatives—'I would be
enraged to find her sandals missing from their place outside her

door, and would hide some precious item from her room, to force a quarrel'[10]—it is evident that the squabbles were both an expression of their intimacy and a less than conscious struggle to deny its increasing appropriation of their hearts. Kadambari's disparaging remarks—'Rabi is the darkest among the brothers and neither is he good-looking. . .He has a peculiar voice and will never be a good singer. . .Satya [the cousin] sings much better. . .He will never be able to write like Bihari Chakraborty'[11]—are attempts at distancing herself from her attraction to him, keeping its dangerous consequences at bay. From his lifelong devotion to her memory, evoked in a number of his poems and songs, it is apparent that Rabi justly registered Kadambari's taunts as teasing, her soulful eyes saying something quite different from her tart tongue.

In the last decade of his life, Rabindranath attempted to recreate elements of his adolescent relationship with another young woman, Rani Mahalanobis. In his letters to her, he is not the serious, even sad-looking man in most of his photographs but displays an impish sense of humour as he seeks to tease the young woman who enjoys the great man's playfulness. With her, he can lay aside the burden of his genius, become a carefree young man or a child demanding maternal ministrations and complaining at their absence, as he did long ago with Kadambari. In her memoir, Rani gives one such instance at the end of a visit to Shantiniketan.

When he asked me why I had decided to leave that day I had to find the excuse of saying that my return ticket was already purchased. He jokingly replied, 'Don't you realize how disrespectful it is towards me if you leave with the excuse that your ticket will be wasted. Is it not more worthwhile to stay over a few days more with me than the price of that ticket? To get my company you can't even afford lose that measly amount?' At last Kobi said, 'Alright, you may go. At the last moment I will have such a severe illness, then I would see how you can leave me. If my "head-nurse" is not there who will take care of me?'

Rani cancelled the ticket and stayed back.[12] But, of course, Rabi was now Rabindranath Tagore, an Indian icon and a world famous writer, and Rani could not ignore that fact for any length of time. He, too, could not completely go back to being the Rabi of yore, ask for a consoling caress or a wordless riffling of her fingers through his hair. He might have wanted to lay his head in her lap but the problem was that she wanted to lay hers in *his* lap.

Kadambari, who had developed a passion for literature, was more than simply an adoring fan of Rabi's poetic and other literary efforts. She was an insightful and at times acerbic critic. And if, in spite of her sentiment for the poet that hugely outweighed her critical observations on his poems, misgivings about his poetic powers sometimes assailed Rabi, 'this was the only field of activity left in which I had any chance of retaining my self-respect, I could not allow the judgment of another to deprive me of all hope; moreover so insistent was the spur within me that to stop my poetic adventure was a matter of sheer impossibility.'[13]

Kadambari, then, was a Muse not only of inspiration but also of affirmation and criticism. She was thus indispensable to the flourishing of Rabi's youthful creativity by providing him both an affective and cognitive support system.[14]

In later life, Rabindranath looked down upon his youthful creations, such as his first published long poem *Kobikahani* (The Poet's Story), which he wrote at the age of sixteen, as effusions of boyhood straining after effect since they were products 'of that age at which a writer has seen practically nothing of the world except an exaggerated image of his own nebulous self'.[15] The earthly Muse for those creations, however, merges with its heavenly counterpart as Kadambari acquires an almost transcendent dimension in the old poet's memory. Thus, in the letter to Andrews in which Rabindranth is expressing his homesickness for India, and from which I quoted in an earlier chapter, it is Kadambari's visage I espy behind the mask of the Jibandebta when he writes of 'my first great sweetheart—my Muse' and grieves:

> But where is this sweetheart of mine who was almost the only companion of my boyhood and with whom I spent my idle days of youth exploring the mysteries of dreamland? She, my Queen, has died and my world has shut against me the door of its inner apartment of beauty which gives one the real taste of freedom.[16]

Some of Rabindranath's biographers have called Kadambari 'the deepest female influence on Rabindranath's youth' '(Dutta and Robinson), 'playmate and guardian angel' (Kriplani), 'deepest heartfelt realization in [Rabindranath's] life' (Bhattacharya). But perhaps what she meant to Rabindranath is best expressed in his own words, even when Kadambari is not their explicit addressee: 'The heart of human beings is like liquid, which changes shape if the containers are different. Very rarely it finds the ideal container where it will not feel the emptiness or constriction.'[17] Kadambari was simply Rabi's ideal container.

As Rabi's adolescence gives way to youth, there is a subtle change in the mood of the relationship. The first hint comes in Rabi's memory of accompanying Jyotirindranath and Kadambari to their garden estate, a small two-storeyed house on the banks of the Ganges. It has begun to rain and Rabi has just composed a tune to the poet Vidyapati's verse.

> Enamelled with melody, that cloudy day on the Ganga shore survives, even now, in the jewel casket of my rain songs. I

remember the gusts of wind that assailed the treetops every now and then, causing a great stirring and swaying among the branches, the dinghies scudding along the river, their white sails tilting in the wind, the splash of tall, plunging waves upon the ghat. When Bouthakrun returned, I sang the song for her. She listened in silence, without uttering a word of praise. I was sixteen or seventeen then. We argued about the pettiest of things, but our exchanges had lost their sharpness.[18]

No longer children, the sexual current in their mutual attraction, and the impossibility of its consummation, had begun to breach the wall standing in the way of its conscious awareness.

The private name Rabi now gave Kadambari was Hecate, the Greek goddess of sorcery and witchcraft, though Rabi owed the name more to Shakespeare than Greek mythology. Intimately familiar with *Macbeth*, which he had translated into Bengali under the guidance of one of his home tutors at the age of thirteen, I can only surmise that it is Hecate's speech (in Act 3, Scene 5) which holds clues to what the name meant for both of them. Chastising the other witches for having given Macbeth riddles and prophecies about his future without telling her—and what is worse, doing all this for a man who behaves like a heedless, wayward brat engrossed in pursuing his own needs—Hecate says that she will now take over and, with her spells, produce spirits that will trick Macbeth with illusions. Fooled into thinking he is greater than fate, he will mock death, and will think he is above wisdom, grace and fear. He would feel safe now, but as we all know security is a mortal's chief enemy. To bewitch is to both seduce and make helpless, but Rabi seems to be referring as much to Kadambari's frequent teasing of him—as the spoilt son who has illusions of grandeur and feels invulnerable—as to the hold her spell has cast on his mind.

Looking back, a middle-aged Rabindranath firmly turns his

back on his youth: 'This period of my life, from fifteen or sixteen to twenty-two or twenty-three, was one of utter disorderliness.'[19] The imagery he uses to condemn the passions of a youthful mind (and the desires of a young man's body, I would add) is charged with distaste and dread of the animality of a powerful adversary who is difficult to tame or even control. 'The swirling passions of the immature mind', he writes, are 'twilit, misshapen and overblown', haunting 'the trackless, nameless wilderness of the mind' like 'giant malformed amphibians [that] moved about the treeless jungles that flourished in the primeval ooze'.[20] These urges torment the mind like a 'fever', are 'maladies', and if confined within the person without being released in some worthwhile work (*sublimated* in modern parlance), poison life.

We need to remember that Rabindranath is writing of a period of life that is under the sway of the purely sexual. We do not know exactly how Rabi's closeness to an attractive young woman, with whom he spent so much time alone together, played out in the conscious and unconscious parts of his mind at a time of life when arousal is unpredictable; merely the chafe of underwear against the genitals is capable of producing an erection, and wet dreams can be shamelessly promiscuous in the female images they conjure. I will speculate—and this is indeed looking through a *speculum* darkly—that some of the tempestuous feelings aroused by the dictates of his own body and the intimacy with Kadambari were consciously denied and vicariously lived through an ardent engagement with English literature.

In his *Reminiscences*, Rabindranath writes of the 'harshness, exuberance and wantonness' in one of his 'literary gods' of the time, Shakespeare, whose plays seek to discover in the core of man's being an ultimate image of his own most violent desire. Distancing himself by forsaking the personal 'I' for the collective 'We', he says:

The spirit of this bacchanalian revelry of Europe found entrance into our demurely well-behaved social world, woke us up, and made us lively. We were dazzled by the glow of unfettered life which fell upon our custom-smothered heart, pining for an opportunity to disclose itself. . .In this wise did the excitement of English literature come to sway the heart of the youth of our time, and at mine the waves of this excitement kept beating from every side. This first awakening is the time for the play of energy, not its repression. . .[21]

Our restricted social life, our narrower field of activity, was hedged in by such monotonous uniformity that tempestuous feelings found no entrance—all was as calm and quiet as could be. So our hearts naturally craved the life-bringing shock of the passionate emotion in English literature. Ours was not the aesthetic enjoyment of literary art, but the jubilant welcome by stagnation of a turbulent wave, even though it should stir up to the surface the slime of the bottom.[22]

As an adult, Rabindranath continued to admire the greats of English literature—Milton, Byron and especially Shakespeare—for their authentic exposure of feelings, but now felt that passion was only one of the ingredients of literature and not its sum. Unlike the best of Sanskrit poetry or drama, English literature exhibited the fury of passion in isolation from nature, snatched away from its context. It brought to the fore the raging fever of human desire, but not the balm of health and repose that encircles it in the universe.[23]

In his youth, though, passion is exciting yet slimy. Rabindranath's acknowledgement of the power of passion, the promptings of desire, and his later dismissal of it as concealer of 'Truth', was not a conclusion he reached simply from a dispassionate analysis of English literature. His ambivalence towards the play of desire in human life has another source that lies in Rabi's less than conscious apprehension

of the turbulence of his own emotions in his relationship with
Kadambari, feelings that were both deliciously exciting and strictly
forbidden. Unheeding of moral and aesthetic considerations, they
made him feel intensely alive yet threatened to undermine all self-
possession.

The relationship with Kadambari had rooted Rabi, seduced him
back into the world, quickened his psyche with the life force of Eros,
given him great joy and affirmed his destiny as a poet; and yet it
inevitably came up against the reality that she belonged to another.
In a letter to Rani Mahalanobis, written when he was almost seventy,
Rabindranath conflates recollections of his late childhood and early
youth into a single memory that is a displaced reference to his Oedipal
experiences and relationships.

Rani, I don't know why suddenly that day a childhood imagery
awoke. Winter morning, around 5.30. Still slightly dark. Like my
usual habit, I came outside early in the morning. Scanty clothes
on, a cotton shirt and briefs. Our childhood was spent in such poor
plight. Was feeling cold inside—so, went to the corner room that
we called 'toshkhana' where the servants stayed. In that half light,
Chinte, Jyotidada's servant was burning coal in iron hooks with a
pan on it, making toast for Jyotida. The room was filled with the
smell of melting butter on those warm toasts. And with that was
Chinte's quiet humming along with the faint warmth from the
burning wood and coal. At that time I think I was about 9. I was
like slippery moss, gently floating over life and family. I still didn't
have any roots anywhere; it was like I was not anyone's—from
morning till night, I was only in the hands of servants, and didn't
have any option of experiencing any loving touch. Jyotida was
married, he had someone to think about him, from early morning
he had his warm toasts going. I was like on the shores of the Padma
[Ganges] of the family, in the land of unlovables—there were no

Rabi, 17, in England.

Rabi as a young man.

Rabi in his early teens.

Rabi's mother, Sharada Devi.

Rabi's father, Debendranath Tagore.

Rabi and his brother, Jyotirindranath

Rabi's brother, Jyotirindranath Tagore.

Rabindranath, 23, with newly
wedded wife Mrinalini.

Rabi's brother, Jyotirindranath and
sister-in-law, Kadambari.

Rabi's sister-in-law, Kadambari.

Rabindranath, 23, with newly wedded wife Mrinalini, 12.

Rabi as a young man.

flowers or fruits or any blossoms there—only lot of free time to sit alone and think. And the shore of the Padma that Jyotida belonged to was green—there would come from afar some smell, some songs, some images of life that caught my eyes. I understood that the truth of the journey of life was there—but I did not have the sail to cross through it. So, I would sit amidst emptiness and keep staring at the sky. From childhood I was far from practical life, so from then 'I am thirsty of the afar' [one of his songs]. Quite without any reason this whole image came alive—then I thought it over. At that time I was like my own shadow, I didn't have any family, there was no meaning in life—there was no love at home, no friendship outside. Jyotidada was the firm truth, *his family was his alone.* At that time it was difficult for me to imagine that someday some of this could also be possible—I could see the image of completeness but couldn't ever think it would have an end. That morning the aroma of warm toasts was the symbol of a complete life—that day there was nothing in my life to stand comparison to that. But where is that morning, that humming of Chinte—and Jyotida, where is he with all of his world? Today in this cold morning, unwanted Robi is set in his ship for the big world—all that was the truth of that time has no sign today, and all the shadow of that time has become so strangely huge. . .[24]

More than fifty years later, the plaint that Jyotirindranath's wife (who constitutes his family, since the couple is childless) is his alone, continues to echo in the chambers of Rabindranath's heart—the smell of warm buttered toast, the symbol of Rabi's exclusion from the fantasized completeness of the 'parental' couple, evoking both longing and resignation.

8

The Passage to England

In early 1878, when Rabi was seventeen years old, Debendranath decided that he be sent to England to study law and then train as a barrister. The thinking in the family seemed to be that the boy was flighty and a layabout. It was time he prepared himself for the seriousness of adult life and stepped into a respectable profession. We have no record of what this decision must have meant to Rabi whose whole sense of his self was anchored in being a poet. The identity of a poet was not a role he had chosen but one that had seized him. It had given a meaning and direction to his life and could only be repudiated at grave psychic peril. We only know that Rabi complied with his father's wishes in the manner of many Indian sons: through a passive-aggressive stance that combines an apparent obedience with silent subversion, in Rabi's case by neglecting his law studies in favour of attending lectures on English literature and returning home without a degree in law.

Before proceeding to England, it was again decided that he first spend a few months with his elder brother Satyendranath so that he could become familiar with Western manners. Satyendranath, an anglicized member of the Indian Civil Service, was a judge in Ahmedabad and Rabi was to accompany him when he left for

England later that year on his furlough, the home leave given to all members of the ICS who were almost all British. Satyendranath, in fact, was the first Indian to be selected for the service that liked to think of itself as the 'steel frame' that held India—the 'jewel in the crown'—together.

Satyendranath's wife and his daughter, Indira Devi, were already in England, awaiting his arrival and Rabi spent three lonely months in the judge's residence. This was a seventeenth century Mughal palace, a large sprawling building in Shahibag on the banks of the river Sabarmati that had once been the residence of the governor of Gujarat, Prince Khurram, later crowned as the Emperor Shah Jahan. Since his brother was away in court during the day, Rabi spent his time alone, polishing his English by reading some of the English books in his brother's library, such as Tennyson's works, with the help of a dictionary. In *Boyhood Days*, he describes his mental state as being that of a plant torn up by the roots and transplanted from one field to another. As an introverted youth, ' In an unfamiliar world that was hard to mingle with but impossible to escape, a boy of my temperament constantly came up against emotional stumbling blocks.'[1] As he had done time and again when caught in unpleasant situations from which there was no escape, Rabi took flight in his imagination. The street outside the palace began to resound to the clatter of hooves as the Turkish cavalry, its spears glinting in sunlight, marched past. In the enclosure above the guard house, shehnai players and their percussionists played ragas appropriate to the time of the day. In the Mughal court, whispered conspiracies were rife. Abyssinian eunuchs, armed with drawn swords, guarded the harem. One could hear the tinkling sounds of armlets and bangles of the begums and fountains of rose water rose high in the seraglio's baths. And, of course, he wrote poems and, as a first, composed music to three of his songs that herald the birth of Rabindrasangeet, perhaps the best loved musical genre of Bengal—at least of its middle classes.

In August, Rabi was packed off to Bombay to live for a month with an anglicized Maharashtrian family before his ship sailed for London. The family's sixteen-year-old daughter, Annapurna, had just returned from England. The idea was to familiarize Rabi with modern young women who were not part of the family, the kind of women he would encounter in England. It was also, as he says, an easy way to learn English.

Thrown together with a pretty girl, Rabi preened like any other young man. He informed Ana that he was a poet and to substantiate his assertion, promptly composed a song with the poetic name he had given her, Nalini, woven in its verses. He then sang the song for her. The maiden was bowled over. 'O Poet!' Rabindranath remembers her exclaiming, 'your song would give me renewed life, I think, even on my dying day.'[2] Ana was also the first girl who openly conveyed to Rabi that he was a handsome youth, in contrast to Kadambari who had always decried Rabi's looks even while she conveyed that she found him attractive in every other way. Shy, dreamy and totally naïve about the ways of a woman's heart, Rabi did not act on Ana's infatuation, as she might have wanted him to. He preferred to remain content with the pleasurable feelings she aroused in him and the boost her admiration gave to his self-confidence as a man. Flirtation is a deferral of consummation—in Rabi's case, a permanent one.

On 20 September 1878, together with his brother Satyendranath, Rabi sailed for England. He was to stay there for some sixteen months. Rabi's English sojourn, which marked the beginning of a lifelong exploration of another duality in his psyche, India–West, also signalled the end of his boyhood. In England, 'I absorbed within myself the fusion of East and West. In my own heart, I discovered the meaning of my name,' are the final sentences of his memoir on his boyhood days.[3]

After the first three months, spent in the shelter of his brother's family who had rented a house in Brighton, Rabindranath went to London to begin his law studies. In his first autobiographical writing, he remembers a 'cruel' London wrapped in a mantle of cold loneliness. Knowing no one who lived nearby and unfamiliar with the topography of the city, he would sit for days at the window of his scantily furnished room, gazing at the grey, wintry outside world. He describes the view from the window in words that could apply equally to his inner world, 'There was a frown on its countenance; the sky was turbid, lacking luster like a dead man's eye; everything seemed turned in upon itself, shunned by the rest of the world.'[4] Yet, little of this gloom is evident in the thirteen letters he wrote back home at the time, many of them to Kadambari, and published in the family periodical *Bharati*.[5] In these letters, at the beginning of his stay, especially the winter months in London, there are indeed complaints about the weather, an 'arrested mobility that cloaks everything', the sun that has 'diminished to a mere hearsay' and how 'In this Land of Darkness all my intellect seems to be wasting away—I cannot write so much so that even composing a letter seems to be beyond me. . .Only after coming to this country have I fully realized the worth of our mornings and evenings, and of our moonlit nights.'[6] By the end of his stay, however, the wintry gloom has given way to summery exuberance. In one of his last letters, from Torquay, a town in Devonshire, he rhapsodizes over its scenic beauty, riverside, fields; he has never seen a place as beautiful as this where 'everything seems to smile'.[7]

That *Jibansmriti* and *Paschatya Bhraman* remember his England sojourn differently is not surprising. The memory of a past period of life is not the result of a deliberate weighing of its highs and lows to reach a considered opinion. The selection of remembered events is also dictated by the memorist's present affective state—in the case of *Jibansmriti,* a fifty-year-old Rabindranath emerging from a long period of mourning. London was certainly another immersion in loneliness, its soil even more inhospitable than that of Ahmedabad.

Yet, what the letters written at the time focus on is not what London denied the seventeen-year-old Rabi but what it granted him: the exhilaration of emerging from a familial cocoon into the wonders of a wider world and, above all, the gratification of being admired and found desirable by the opposite sex, thus consolidating a masculine identity that had seemed vulnerable in his latency years.

Full of wit and verve, and marked by sharp observations of English life, the travelogue constituted by these letters is a fine piece of writing and remains an exceptionally percipient comparison of Indian and Western mores. What makes the travelogue even more remarkable is that it is penned by a seventeen-year-old and, for me, it is a more conclusive evidence of Rabindranath's genius than his early poems. Rabindranath himself was reluctant to publish these letters in the form of a book, which besides its literary value also has the distinction of being the first Bengali book written in the colloquial language. He deplores precisely what lends the letters their verve: his youthful audacity, unmindful of political correctness. His reluctance had perhaps also to do with his concern about his legacy. In the 1936 preface to the book, he writes that he is pleased to discover an underlying respect covering the wild profusion of disrespect to which his youthful self was prone: 'This is because I wholeheartedly despise the art of skillful and caustic derision. The capacity to love is God's best gift to mankind. I have never accepted the enticement offered by literature's scandalmongers—if nothing else, this is a fact about me that I would like to leave behind.'[8]

Rabindranath was impatient with Rabi's inclination to bravado. He was also dismissive of seventeen-year-old Rabi's belief, shared by many a youth, that he was unique, where 'One has to say "I am not like others, there is nothing anywhere that is fit for me to admire". I was then too young to realize that this is a sign of poor intellect and proof of foolish immaturity.'[9] In Rabi's very first letter to Kadambari, we see an instance of what Rabindranath finds galling in his younger

self. Landing in Brindisi in Italy and stepping on European soil for
the first time, Rabi writes to her:

> You are aware of my imaginative nature; I had thought a
> marvellous sight would open up in front of my eyes as soon
> as I reached Europe! This must remain in my fantasies and can
> never be expressed in words. But I have seen since childhood that
> reality and imagination rarely match. I am unable, due to a flaw
> in my nature, to fully experience many things. Before arriving in
> a new country, I imagine its newness in such a way that once I am
> there, it does not seem new anymore; before seeing any grand
> spectacle, I imagine it to be so grand that in reality it does not
> seem grand anymore. That Europe did not seem so novel to me
> made everyone speechless![10]

But very soon, the authentic face of a wide-eyed youth emerges from
the put-on mask of an all-knowing adult. On the train journey from
Brindisi to Paris, Rabi enthuses over the beautiful landscape, 'like
a poet's dream', with its marvellous vineyards, mountains, rivers,
lakes, cottages, tiny villages: 'It was as if we were reading poetry
all the way.'[11]

What strikes me about Rabi's first three letters to Kadambari is
the pains he takes to assure her that he is not attracted to English
girls, even when they are beautiful. On the ship there are only older
women, one too tall, her lips askew, face scarred, teeth prominent.
Another is like a geometric line without width: elongated body,
elongated face, elongated hands and legs. The only young woman on
the ship sits in a far corner of the deck with her Bible, a veil drawn
over her face. And in any case, he is by nature fearful of women,
and keeps his distance from them.[12] In the second letter, Rabi mocks
English women as dressed-up performing dolls: 'I could not bear
these ways intended to captivate men—the gestures, the studied

lilting tones, the sweet smiles. I do not think anyone can captivate me by these mannerisms and gestures.'[13] It is unknown how Kadambari received these protestations, whether she accepted them at face value or whether, with the famed feminine intuition reputed to be especially acute in matters of the heart, sensed that her dear Rabi 'doth protest too much'.

The next letter begins with description of a fancy-dress ball to which Rabi went dressed as a Bengali landowner in gold-embroidered velvet joba and a velvet turban. Rabi's description alternates between his enjoyment of the event, his excitement, and their denial that seems designed to appease Kadambari and lull any suspicions she might harbour.

> The room was packed with pretty faces—wherever I stepped were ladies' gowns, and wherever I looked my eyes were bedazzled. . .Smiles played on lips, the ladies fired away relentlessly and without hesitation, using every manner of arsenal available to win hearts. But do not be afraid—our stony hearts were not even scratched.[14]

The letter continues with another dance party to which Rabi has been invited and we discover that Rabi likes to dance the 'gallop', the 'lancers' and perhaps even the waltz, the quadrille and the polka, which were fixtures on the programmes of English balls in the late nineteenth century. Here, too, the sensual quickening and its disavowal stand out in sharp relief.

> We entered the room, which was brilliant with gaslight, but compared to the radiant beauty of hundreds of young women, the gaslight seemed to fade. The room was bright and filled with laughter. It was a celebration of beauty—the eyes were bedazzled upon entering the room.[15]

After a description of English dances and the etiquette governing
the dancing, such as the introductions by the hostess and filling in
the names of the partners for the various dances on a dance card,
he proceeds:

> It seems as if everyone is spinning around delirious with joy.
> Rhythmically the music plays, and rhythmically the feet move.
> The room has become quite warm and what can one say about
> the great surge of excitement. A dancing couple likes each other
> tremendously and their lips can scarcely contain their smiles. .
> .A dance ends, the music stops, the gentleman escorts his weary
> partner. A table is laden with fruit, cakes and wine. Perhaps they
> partake of the refreshments or perhaps they retire to a secluded
> part of the garden for an amorous tete-a-tete.[16]

He himself is less than a wholehearted participant in the revelry
of the dance parties, he assures Kadambari, leaving the unasked
question suspended between them, 'Then why do you go?'

> I am not inordinately fond of these dance invitations. To twirl
> around madly in that fashion with an unfamiliar girl is something
> I really do not like. I quite like dancing with those whom I am
> familiar with. I knew Miss Such-and-such quite well, and she was
> quite nice to look at, and which is why when I danced the gallop
> with her, I made no mistakes. But I danced the lancers with Miss
> Such-and-such, and since I did not know her, and she was terrible
> to look at. . .I committed every possible kind of sin while dancing
> with her.[17]

And if tempted, Rabi is quick to resist the temptation.

> I once had a beautiful partner. I had tried my best not to dance with

her. But after much persuasion from our hostess, I had perforce
to descend onto the dance floor where I somehow completed the
dance and then bolted![18]

Rabi took pains to deny that he was attracted to English girls; dusky
Bengali girls were far more enticing. At the same dance party, on
seeing a dark face, 'My heart leapt when I saw her. It is difficult to
say how much I fancied her! I walked around, desperate to make
her acquaintance at any cost. Just think how long it was since I had
seen a dark face! In that gathering of fair-skinned ladies, my soul
was drawn towards that sweet, dusky face as by a magnet.' He is
devastated when he learns that the girl is an Anglo-Indian, of mixed
English and Indian blood, a community scorned by both the British
and upper class Indians, and foregoes making her acquaintance.

By the end of his stay, and especially after living for a few months
as a boarder with Dr Scott and his family—whose two young
daughters promptly fell in love with him[19]—a much more confident
Rabi is voicing unabashed admiration for aspects of Western culture
which he would dearly want his countrymen to possess: the lack of
servility in the servants, the respect for talent and, above all, certain
features of family life and the high place of women in social life.
From the passion and the length of his diatribes on the shortcomings
of the Indian family, it is apparent that the West had become his ally
in voicing some of his own discontents while growing up in the
extended Tagore family.

We do not give the name of servitude to slavery within the family,
but we can at the most gild it with a name and transform the
iron fetters of discipline into those of gold, but cannot erase its
restrictions—the harmful effects persist. I had once thought that
Hindus were by nature simple and spontaneous, without any
unnatural restrictive laws. But I am ashamed to say that any more.

Hindus without unnatural laws? Just peep into their families! Just look at the rigidity between brother and sister, mother and father, men and women. . .It is even forbidden for one to talk too much or even laugh in front of one's elders. How terrible! If you cannot talk freely to those with whom you spend twenty-four hours of the day, cannot laugh heartily, if in their presence you have to rein your tongue in, place a weight on your happy countenance and wear a mask of reverence the livelong day, where then do you go for your relaxation?. . .English homes have a feeling of cheerful relaxation. Parents, brothers and sisters, wives and sons gather around the fireplace and cheer it up with their happy talk, laughter and singing. After a hard day's work, one returns home to a sense of joy and familiarity. [In India]. . .in one room, the father-in-law, along with his clutch of elderly friends, sits drawing on the hookah, and blames today's generation and its unholy behaviour for the impending onset of divine recrimination; in another room sits the bride of the house, her veil drawn over her face, silently listening to her mother-in-law ladling out to her her daily dose of blame; in another room, her husband along with his young friends gossip maliciously—no one in England could imagine such a scenario. Our freedom of speech is with other people. . .In our families, we have to make strangers our own, because our own are strangers to us.[20]

And in his praise of middle class English women who play an active part in Western social life, we hear echoes of his frustrations around the confinement of women in the *andar mahal.*

These [English] women are not confined to the house; they converse with friends and at meetings when superior matters are discussed, they listen and may voice their own opinions. . . In the presence of people, a very happy and pleased expression is presented; although she herself may not be a witty person, she enjoys a good joke, is generous with her praise if there is something she likes, and laughs heartily if she hears something amusing. It is not ideal behavior for women here to keep their lips sealed or to be overcome with shyness. . .A bit of reticence is not unpleasing to the eye, one may even see some poetic sweetness in it—but to deal with shyness the livelong day is painful indeed. If one is rewarded with an answer to one's question after two or three hours of perseverance, one can bear it once—but if one is brought to the brink of exhaustion each day in trying to get her to say a few words, it would then be difficult to survive. If you cannot share a joke with me without inhibition, I would be forced to dissociate myself from you and look for other company. The 'mantras' chanted at the wedding ceremony will not magically give rise to love; marriage by itself does not lead to love. If no love exists between my wife and I, and furthermore if my wife cannot keep me entertained with lively conversation, will I not look for sources of amusement elsewhere, leaving my mute lady companion behind?[21]

I can imagine the consternation with which such sentiments were received in the Tagore family. Commenting on similar advocacy of a freer intercourse between the sexes in Rabi's next letter, Dwijendranath, the eldest brother and editor of the family journal *Bharati*, observed:

Women can never share with men the kind of conversation they have with friends of their own sex in the inner recesses of the house. The presence of a man in their midst would only mar their enjoyment. This is why the outer parts of the houses have been created for men to gather together and converse in, and the inner recesses for women. . .If you were to ask, 'Where is the harm in

the opposite sexes meeting for a friendly exchange?', the answer
would be that gradually it would evolve that friendship between
males and that between females would be termed as inferior, and
glances exchanged between friends of the opposite sexes would
be termed as a superior friendship. Its proof being the way the
hearts of European women leap at the prospect of dancing with
men at balls![22]

Alarmed at Rabi's radical questioning of family and social values,
and coupled with the fact that he was not making any headway in
his law studies, Debendranath decreed that Rabi return on the same
ship that was bringing his brother's family back to India.

Rabindranath never lost his attraction for the West and what it gave
him: a quickening of the mind in the company of other searching and
alive minds who appreciated what he had to offer. The West never
became his world, yet he remained grateful for the gift of acceptance
and love he had received from it. In October 1913, he writes to
Andrews, 'In India the range of our lives is narrow and discontinuous,
that is the reason why our minds are beset with provincialism.'[23]

And from London, in July 1920:

When I am in the West I feel more strongly than ever I am received
in a living world of mind. I miss here my sky and light and leisure,
but I am in touch with those who feel and express their need of
me and whom I can offer myself. Our span of life is short and
opportunity rare, so let us sow our seeds of thought where the
soil claims them, where the harvest will ripen.[24]

As with the influential art historian Ananda Coomaraswamy and
Mahatama Gandhi, it was the long (and essential) exposure to the
West that enabled Rabindranath to make seminal contributions to
the dialogue of civilizations.

Rabindranath believed that the East–West encounter initiated by colonialism had so far been confined to the surface. In spite of its terrible violence and inequities, he professed to discern at the heart of this encounter the coming together of the *ideas* of the West and India ('My India is an Idea and not a geographical expression'[25]), seeds that would germinate and mature in a great future union.

Rabi's stay in England was to initiate a lifelong preoccupation with the duality of India (or, later and more generally, the East) and the West. His observations on India's encounter with the West, its consequences and its ideal outcome, remain unsurpassed in depth of insight. In his reflections on this encounter, Rabindranath was incisive on the disquiets afflicting both the Indian and Western civilizations, disquiets which have become raging discontents in our own times. At the outset, let me first say that I am in substantial agreement with Rabindranath in positing an Indian civilization that has features which distinguish it from Western civilization.

The main river in Indian culture, Rabindranath says, has flowed in four streams: the Vedic, the Puranic, the Buddhist and the Jain.

It has its source in the heights of the Indian consciousness. But a river, belonging to a country, is not fed by its own waters alone. . . The Muhammadan, for example, has repeatedly come into India from outside, laden with his own stores of knowledge and feeling and his wonderful religious democracy, bringing freshet after freshet to swell the current. To our music, our architecture, our pictorial art, our literature, the Muhammadans have made their permanent and precious contribution. Those who have studied the lives and writings of our medieval saints, and all the great religious movements that sprang up in the time of the Muhammadan rule, know how deep is our debt to this foreign current that has so intimately mingled with our life.[26]

Then there are other currents: the Sikh, the Zoroastrian but also the Chinese, Japanese and Tibetan, for India did not remain isolated.

> Side by side with them must finally be placed the Western culture. For only then shall we be able to assimilate this last contribution to our common stock. A river flowing within banks is truly our own, and it can contain its due tributaries; but our relations with a flood can only prove disastrous.[27]

Rabindranath believes, as I do, in the existence of an overarching Indian identity, in spite of the many surface differences, which have perhaps been magnified by the discipline of social anthropology that by its very nature is attuned to look at individual trees rather than espying the pattern of the forest. Rabindranath, of course, writes of this much more eloquently than I ever could.

> The bringing about of an intellectual unity in India is, I am told, difficult to the verge of impossibility owing to the fact that India has so many different languages. Such a statement is as unreasonable as to say that man, because he has a diversity of limbs should find it impossible to realize life's unity, and that only an earthworm composed of a tail and nothing else could truly know that it had a body.[28]

He then goes on to compare India with Europe, which has a common civilization, with an intellectual unity which is not based on uniformity.

What is the defining feature of Indian civilization according to Tagore whose loss is responsible for much of its contemporary disquiet? And I use the word 'contemporary' deliberately for both Tagore's and our times, since the situation, if it has changed in the last one hundred years, has done so only for the worse. According to Tagore, the defining feature of Indian civilization, which we are in the process of losing, is sympathy. Sympathy, as I understand it, is the feeling of kinship that extends to beyond what is our kin, a sense of 'we' that extends beyond kinship. And this feeling of kinship is not limited to human beings but extends to the natural world. Here Tagore and Gandhi are in complete agreement. 'Brotherhood,' Gandhi writes in one letter, 'is just now a distant aspiration. To me it is a test of true spirituality. All our prayers, and observances are empty nothings so long as we do not feel a live kinship with all life.'[29] To one of his many critics—and there were many throughout his life and even after his death—who wrote to him suggesting that violence is the law of nature and that man is animal first and human afterwards, Gandhi replies that man can be classed as animal only so long as he *retains* his humanity and goes on to say:

> The correspondent apologizes for suggesting that I might regard myself as a remote cousin of the ape. The truth is that my ethics not only permit me to claim but require me to own kinship with not merely the ape but the horse and the sheep, the lion and the leopard, the snake and the scorpion. . .The hard ethics which rule my life, and I hold ought to rule that of every man and woman, impose this unilateral obligation upon us.[30]

For Rabindranath, in contrast to the West, Indian civilization sought to establish a relation with the world, with nature as also with the living beings, not through the cultivation of power but the fostering of sympathy.

> When we know this world as alien to us, then its mechanical aspect takes prominence in our mind; and then we set up our machines and our methods to deal with it and make as much profit as our knowledge of its mechanism allows us to do so.'

This view of things does not play us false. . .this aspect of truth cannot be ignored; it has to be known and mastered. Europe has done so and reaped a rich harvest. . .For us the highest purpose of this world is not merely living in it, knowing it and making use of it, but realizing our own selves in it through expansion of our sympathy; not alienating ourselves from it and dominating it, but comprehending and uniting it with ourselves in perfect union.[31]

In a letter to Andrews, Rabindranath articulates the ideas of India and the West through an 'origin myth'.

From the beginning of their history the Western races have had to deal with nature as their antagonist. This fact has emphasized in their mind the dualistic aspect of truth, the eternal conflict between good and evil. Thus West has kept up the spirit of fight in the heart of their civilization. They seek victory and cultivate power.

The environment in which the Aryan immigrants found themselves in India was that of the forest. The forest, unlike the desert or rock or sea, is living; it gives shelter and nourishment to life. In such a surrounding the ancient forest dwellers of India realized the spirit of harmony with the universe, and emphasized in their mind the monistic aspect of truth. They sought the realization of their soul through the union with all. The spirit of fight and the spirit of harmony, both have their importance in the scheme of things. For making a musical instrument, the obduracy of materials has to be forced to yield to the purpose of the instrument-maker. But music itself is a revelation of beauty, it is not an outcome of fight; it springs from an inner realization of harmony. The musical instrument and music both have their utmost importance for humanity. The civilization that conquers for man, and the civilization that realizes for him the fundamental unity in the depth of existence, are complementary to each other.

> When they join hands human nature finds its balance and its
> pursuits through their rugged paths attain their ultimate meaning
> in an ideal of perfection.[32]

The ideas of the two civilizations, when articulated through history, have picked up dross and it is now through the distortions and perversions of their core ideas that the civilizations encounter each other. If the caste idea and the suffering of the excluded is an Indian distortion, then the perversion of the Western idea of the conquest of nature, with its marvellous training of the intellect, is the passion for wealth and power. This passion has not only science as its ally but also such forces as nation worship and idealization of organized selfishness. Nationalism, for Rabindranath, was collective selfishness, collective narcissism—deeply inimical to the idea of sympathy. Rabindranath is prophetic when he talks of the passion for wealth:

> The whole of the human world, throughout its length and breadth,
> has felt the gravitational pull of a giant planet of greed, with
> concentric rings of innumerable satellites, causing in our society
> a marked deviation from the moral orbit.[33]

A person, whether in the West or the East, who has unreservedly embraced the idea of the West, together with its cult of power and idolatry of money, has, 'in a great measure, reverted to his primitive barbarism, a barbarism whose path is lit by the lurid light of intellect. For barbarism is the simplicity of a superficial life. It may be bewildering in its surface adornments and complexities, but it lacks the ideal to impart to it the depth of moral responsibility.'[34]

The future combination of the ideas of the West and India could not come to fruition as long as the relationship between the two remained that of victor and vanquished, the giver and the receiver.

A realization of the complementarity of the two ideas required that Indians first became aware of their heritage, of the spirit or mind of India:

> 'Once upon a time we were in possession of such a thing as our own mind in India. It was living. It thought, it felt, it expressed itself.'[35] The wholesale acceptance of modern, Western education has suppressed this mind. It has been treated like a wooden library shelf to be loaded with volumes of second-hand information; 'In consequence, it has lost its own colour and character, and has borrowed polish from the carpenter's shop. . .we have bought our spectacles at the expense of our eyesight.'[36]

And, further:

> If we were to take it for granted, what some people maintain, that Western culture is the only source of light for our mind, then it would be like depending for daybreak upon some star, which is the sun of a far distant sphere. The star may give us light, but not the day; it may give us direction in our voyage of exploration, but it can never open the full view of truth before our eyes. In fact, we can never use this cold starlight for stirring the sap in our branches, and giving colour and bloom to our life. . .[37]

Without a revival of the idea of India, of an Indian-ness or Indian identity in modern parlance, India 'will allow her priceless inheritance to crumble into dust, and trying to replace it clumsily with feeble imitations of the West, make herself superfluous, cheap and ludicrous'.[38]

Such a fate may not be looked at with equanimity. In a globalized world that links not only entertainment and capital flows but also ideas, the bankruptcy of the East will also have an impact on the

Western mind, make it poorer. To adapt Rabindranath's words, if the great light of culture becomes extinct in the East, the horizon in the West will mourn in darkness.

Rabindranath's was not a defensive and regressive repudiation of Western culture.

> Let me say that I have no distrust of any culture because of its foreign character. On the contrary, I believe that the shock of such extraneous forces is necessary for the vitality of our intellectual nature. . .the European culture has come to us, not only with its knowledge, but with its velocity.
>
> Then, again, let us admit that modern science is Europe's great gift to humanity for all time to come. We, in India, must claim it from her hands, and gratefully accept it to be saved from the curse of futility by lagging behind. We shall fail to reap the harvest of the present age if we delay.[39]

What Rabindranath objected to was the disproportional space Western ideas and world view occupied in the modern Indian mind, and thus killed or hampered the opportunity to create a new combination of truths.

> It is this which makes me urge that all the elements in our own culture have to be strengthened, not to resist the Western culture, but truly accept and assimilate it; to use it for our sustenance, not as our burden; to get mastery over this culture and not to live on its outskirts as the hewers of texts and drawers of book learning.[40]

Unlike Gandhi, Rabindranath welcomed modern science and Western forms of knowledge. He admired the fullness of intellectual vigour in the West that is working towards the solution of all problems of life. What he bemoaned is that the mental vitality of modern forms of knowledge are not balanced by the Indian idea of the cultivation of sympathy.

Sympathy, as I understand it, is the highest manifestation of the human soul. It is a continuum of loving connectedness—to nature, art, visions of philosophy or science, living creatures and, of course, to other human beings. For some, it is in the moments of connectedness with the world, its sights, sounds, smells, the radiance of its days and the darkness of its nights, the sap of its trees and plants and the joys and sufferings of its living beings, when they sense and surrender to the spontaneity of sympathy. For others, sympathy is sensed in a feeling of deep connectedness in presence of great art, in the solemnity of sacred spaces or even glimpsed in the aftermath of the sexual embrace when the bodies have separated and are lying together side by side, but are not yet two in their responses. It is in such moments that we sense sympathy as a hidden power in our selves that is not self-centred and is a source of our highest self. These are moments of quiet exaltation that come from the flow of sympathy, of connectedness and communion, to be sharply differentiated from the gratifying boost given by the feeling of power that comes from understanding the world.

Personally, I fully subscribe to Tagore's view that all our poetry, philosophy, science, literature, art, religion, society and politics, serve (or must serve) to widen the range of our kinship, our sympathy, the principle of the soul. Initiated in our love for those who nurtured us when we were children and our own love for our children, friends, lovers as we get older, it is only the wider and wider manifestations of sympathy that are the true measure of human progress. The soul is insignificant as long as it is imprisoned within an individual self. It reveals its significance and its joy only in sympathy, in loving connectedness. The more vigorous our individuality, the less the need to encase the individual self in an armour of self-aggrandizement and more the capacity to make it permeable and thus participate in the play of the soul. To me, the question of the fate of the soul after death, central for our religions, is not especially interesting. If we do not free the soul from its prison of individual self, guarded by warders of self-centredness, while alive, I doubt whether there is such a thing as the soul's freedom, or its salvation, after death. To adapt the poet Robert Frost's observation on love, the earth is the only place for the soul, I don't know where it is likely to get better.

How would the cultivation of sympathy, the defining idea of Indian civilization, work in practice? Let me take a few examples.

Modern psychology, Western in its orientation, has made great advances in uncovering the mysteries of the human mind, the complexity of the human psyche. The truths it has arrived at (valuable as they are), are, however, partial truths. They largely look at a human being from two angles. The first is that the person is a body, a brain / mind entity in psychological terms, and thus they seek to understand psyche through psychologies that derive from biology. The brain / mind school enjoys considerable vogue in contemporary psychology. The other focus of psychology is interpersonal, that is, psyche is understood as a product of experiences, beginning with the family with a person's social groups. As I said, I have no quarrel with the proposition that lies at the heart of modern psychology—that at every moment of his being, a person is a part of his bodily and social orders. What I would like to add—a dimension that I find largely missing from West-inspired psychology—is that a person is not only a part of his bodily and social orders but also of his cosmic order. What I am saying is that if we want to progress further in understanding human mind and behaviour, then besides the *soma* (the body) and the *polis* (the social order), we need to take into account and focus on another partial truth, the *cosmos*.

Cosmos, as I visualize it, has two aspects: one subtle and the other, well, earthy. The subtle aspect of cosmos is the 'spiritual' order which has been variously conceptualized by different cultures at various times of history as animated by gods, ancestral spirits, demonic beings or, in more sophisticated formulations, as God, Universal Spirit or simply the Sacred. The earthy aspect of cosmos is the environment in which we are born and live our lives. Although a few psychologists have sought to link psychological processes with the spiritual order, a systematic study of the effect of environment—nature of terrain, quality of air, sunlight, birds, animals, trees and flowers, seasons and so on—on human development, cognition and mental health has still to be initiated, an area of psychology that naturally evolves from and is uniquely suited to the empathetic spiritual atmosphere and idea of India.[41]

Let me take another hypothetical example, this time from psychotherapy: the treatment of a patient suffering from anhedonia, the condition where one finds no pleasure in any activity, however intrinsically pleasurable the activity may be. In a psychotherapy imbued with the idea of India, the therapeutic goal will not only be a restoration of sexual pleasure, but a restoration that takes place under the guiding star of loving intimacy (the form of sympathy in this context) which transforms the sex into a thing of beauty, of truth—a glimpse of *sat-chit-ananda*. In Indian psychotherapy, the pleasure of eating will not be restored only for itself but under the star of fellowship (the form of sympathy in this particular context), which turns even a simple meal into a feast, a celebration of solidarity with others who share it.

Similarly, Rabindranath's vision would also raise questions about literature. Have we sufficiently explored the basic assumptions that lie behind Western theories of literary criticism and judgements of literary worth, which we use in the teaching of literature in our Indian universities? Do they need to be balanced, or at least looked at from the angle of empathy which, following Rabindranath, I have postulated as the defining feature of Indian civilization, the idea of India? A hint of the possibilities is again provided by Rabindranath in his remarks on Shakespeare, who he greatly admired, and Kalidasa, who he revered.

> The fury of passion in two of Shakespeare's youthful poems is exhibited in conspicuous isolation. It is snatched away, naked, from the context of the All; it has not the green earth or the blue sky around it; it is there ready to bring to our view the raging fever which is in man's desires, and not the balm of health and repose which encircles it in the universe.[42]

As I understand him, Indian literary criticism will pay as much attention to the movement of sympathy in a work of literature as, following Western canons, it does to the movement of passions. The characters in the Hindi writer Premchand's fiction (or for that matter, Rabindranath's), for example, may not plumb the depth of human passions, a shortcoming that from the Indian point of view is relieved and compensated by the exquisite movement of sympathy that characterizes the best of these works. The highest accolades will, of course, be reserved for literary works that combine both the movements; some of Tolstoy's writings come immediately to mind.

Today social movements in service of justice for the weak and the oppressed are rapidly picking up pace in our country, shaking traditional hierarchies and power structures. This is a welcome development. Most of these movements, however, seem to operate on the basis of only one ethic, *justice*, which is related to the issue of power, of correcting skewed and unfair power relations. In an almost sacralized ethic of justice, what matters is the outcome, not the path. Thus there have been eloquent voices that have defended violence in service of justice. In her *Reflections on Violence*, the philosopher Hannah Arendt writes:

. . .under certain circumstances violence, which is to act without
argument or speech and without reckoning with consequences,
is the only possibility of setting the scales of justice right again. .
.In this sense, rage and the violence that sometimes, not always,
goes with it belong to the 'natural' emotions, and to cure man of
them would mean nothing less than to dehumanize or emasculate
him.[43]

I believe that the Indian ethic of sympathy—compassion in this
context—must temper the quest for justice. In our quest to right a
wrong, bring the ethic of justice to the forefront, we are in danger
of losing sight of what Gandhi and Rabindranath held was the
defining characteristic of Indian civilization. In Rabindranath's
words, 'Creative force needed for the true union in human society
is love; justice is only an accompaniment to it, like the beating of
tom-tom to song.'[44]

Tagore's creation of a university at Shantiniketan in the 1920s
sprang from this vision of India, an Indian university in which Indian
cultures would be represented in all their variety, a university that
would give new life to the idea of India. He soon realized that his
mission was actually much broader. Indeed, it was the mission of
the present age: a meeting of East and West that would bear new
fruit for humanity. Shantiniketan would bring forth its fullness of
flower and fruit only if, through Rabindranath, it also sent its roots
into the Western soil.

At a time of struggle for freedom from Western colonial
domination, a time when Gandhi's call of non-cooperation with
the British was loud, Rabindranath's vision of a harmony between
ideas of East and West for the creation of a universal man had few
takers. He was accused by some of staying apart from the national
struggle, even of toadying to the British, accusations that caused him
deep anguish. Writing to Andrews about his forthcoming travel to

Europe at a time when Gandhi's movement of non-cooperation with the Raj had captured the country's imagination, he says:

> Personally I do not think my overcautious doctor was wise in holding me back. He does not fully realize how great is the mental strain that my stay in India imposes upon me. It is the moral loneliness which is a constant and invisible burden that oppresses me most. I wish it were possible for me to join hands with Mahatma Gandhi and thus at once surrender myself to the current of popular approbation. But I can no longer hide it from myself that we are radically different in our apprehension and pursuit of truth. Today to disagree with Mahatma and yet find rest in one's surroundings in India is not possible and therefore I am waiting for my escape next March with an impatient feeling of longing. I know I have friends in Europe who are my real kindred and whose sympathy will act as a true restorative in my present state of weariness.[45]

It was not as if Rabindranath did not admire Gandhi. In the beginning, he may have called Gandhi a 'moral tyrant' who, in the context of life in his newly established Sabarmati ashram, had the power to make his ideas—on celibacy, food and so on— prevail through strict obedience, through slavery rather than freedom.[46] Later, though, it was precisely the lived morality of Gandhi's life that insisted on following 'truth' as the Mahatma saw it at the moment—his moral power—which evoked Rabindranath's respect and admiration. Where he continued to differ with Gandhi was in their attitudes towards the West. Unlike a young Gandhi's vehement denunciation of Western civilization in his *Hind Swaraj*, Rabindranath only rejected the deformations in the idea of the West that came to India 'all plan and purpose', with the 'shock of passion' and without any humanity. Writing in the wake of the Jalianwala Bagh massacre in Amritsar in which British troops fired on unarmed protesters, killing hundreds—an event

that prompted Gandhi to start a civil disobedience movement and
Tagore to return his knighthood to the British crown—he states his
differences with Gandhi clearly:

> Stung by insult or injustice, we try to repudiate Europe, but
> by doing it we insult ourselves. Let us have the dignity not to
> quarrel or retaliate, not to pay back in smallness with being small
> ourselves. What Gandhi is inculcating in his pugnacious spirit
> of resentment ['revenge' is crossed out] is the withdrawal of
> service from the government. It is a wasteful diversion of the best
> part of our energy to a course which ends in a mere emptiness
> of negation. This is the time when we should dedicate all our
> resources of emotion, thought and character to the service of
> our country in a positive direction. . .
>
> . . .the moral fervour which the life of Gandhi represents and
> which he, of all other men in the world, can call up, is needed. That
> such a precious treasure of power should be put in to the mean and
> frail vessel of our politics allowing it to sail across endless waves of
> angry recrimination is terribly unfortunate for our country where
> our mission is to revive the dead with the fire of soul. . .it is not
> that I do not feel anger in my heart for injustice and insult heaped
> upon my motherland. But this anger of mine should be turned into
> the fire of love. . .India can live and grow by spreading abroad, not
> the political India, but the ideal India. Our Shantiniketan is for this
> mission. We must fully know this ideal India and then will come
> the time when we shall be able to carry her abroad and once again
> her history will find fulfillment in the present age.[47]

The vision of harmony of East and West that had been vouchsafed
to him as an eighteen-year-old in England, the discovery of the
meaning of his name and the mission it imposed upon him—these
were to stay with Rabi till the end of his life.

9

The Falling of the Shadow

On his return from England in March 1880, Rabi effortlessly slipped back into his earlier life, presided over by his brother and Kadambari, embracing its riches of poetry, music and intimacy with an even greater fervour than before.

> In our house, at that time, a cascade of musical emotion was gushing forth day after day, hour after hour, its scattered spray reflecting into our being the whole gamut of rainbow colours. . .
>
> We wrote , we sang, we acted. We poured ourselves out on every side.[1]

He began writing a novel, *Bahuthakuranir Hat* (The Young Queen's Market), wrote poems, songs and a musical play, *Valmiki Pratibha,* which was performed on the terrace of the Jorasanko house in which Rabi also played the lead role. This was followed by another musical, *Kal Mrigaya* (The Fateful Hunt). *Bhagnahriday* (The Broken Heart), a long poem he had begun writing in the latter part of his stay in England, was published in 1881. It brought him certain renown and a lifelong admirer in the Maharaja of Tripura who would later financially contribute to the setting up of Rabindranath's dream

project of an international university in Shantiniketan. Rabindranath
was scathing in his comments on his own youthful poems—'more
sentiment than substance', 'trivial'—and mocked the enthusiasm of
those who immediately christened him the Shelley of Bengal. *The
Broken Heart* was dedicated to Lady He, that is, Kadambari.

From 1880 to 1884, the intensity of Rabi's relationship with
Kadambari and his brother was at its peak, and the vigour he felt
in composing the two musicals could never be matched again.
There was a small blip in the intensity of Rabi's lived life when
Debendranath made another attempt to send him back to England
to continue his law studies. When the ship berthed at Madras Rabi
and a cousin who was accompanying him left the boat and took
the train back to Calcutta. He was summoned to Mussoorie in the
Himalayas where Debendranath was staying at the time; we do not
know how the conversation between father and son proceeded. We
only know that no further attempts were made to persuade Rabi to
follow a respectable profession.

Back in Calcutta, Rabi immediately went to join Jyotirindra and
Kadambari at their riverside villa in Chandernagore where the couple
was staying for a while. Away from Jorasanko and thus shielded from
intrusions of other family members, their intimacy was undisturbed.
He went swimming in the river while Kadambari watched from the
bank. The two spent hours in the woods collecting berries. Rabi's
memory of those days and nights, 'languid with joy, piquant with
yearning', is like a precious gem locked up in a safe in a velvet case,
to be taken out and cherished in times of psychic impoverishment.

These riverside days of mine passed by like consecrated lotus
blossoms floating in the sacred stream. Some rainy afternoons
I spent in a veritable frenzy, singing old Vaishnava songs to
my own tunes, accompanying myself on a harmonium. Other
afternoons we would drift along in a boat, my brother Jyotirindra

accompanying my singing on his violin. Beginning with Raga
Puravi, we went on varying our ragas with the declining day, and
saw, on reaching Raga Behag, that the western sky had pulled
down the shutters on its storehouse of golden playthings, and the
moon had risen in the east.

    Then we would row back to the landing-steps of the villa and
seat ourselves on the quilt spread on the terrace facing the river.
A silvery peace by then rested on both land and water. . .²

Together with the six-year-old's memory of the view of the inner
garden from the servants' quarters—of 'sunlight touching the top of
the coconut row through the pale mist of a severe autumn morning
and the storm-laden rain-clouds rolling up from some abyss behind
the horizon'—the eighteen-year-old Rabi's memory of 'silvery peace'
on the vast expanse of a river were to become recurrent images in
Rabindranath's landscapes.

    There is an elegiac quality to the memory of days and nights in
the villa on the riverbank, perhaps because it stands for the last time
they would be so happy together; it signals the end of an era in Rabi's
and Kadambari's lives. My association to this image of tranquility is
of a swan gliding gracefully on the surface while paddling furiously
underwater, the latter activity invisible to onlookers on the bank.
Rabi's serenity has an undertow of turbulence, 'a veritable frenzy'.
Writing later of the poems collected in *Chhobi O Gaan* (Pictures and
Songs)—which were composed in 1882 and published in the spring
of the following year—Rabindranath says that he was almost mad
during this period, overwhelmed by the gushing floodtide of his
newly awakened youth, and further adds that the kind of restlessness
he experiences on reading this particular collection, even now, has no
counterpart when he returns to any of his other youthful writings.³
In these poems, Rabi has harnessed the chaos of his passions to (in
Nietzsche's phrase) 'give birth to a dancing star' without regarding

it, as he was later often wont to do, as an enemy to be tamed.

The turbulence is not Rabi's alone but is shared by the other two in the threesome, though they register it with different degrees of sensitivity, awareness and capacities for articulation. Each of the three is struggling with his or her own demons but, because of their physical and emotional closeness, is also affected by the inner conflicts of the others. Or to change the metaphor, the brew each one is drinking becomes more bitter because of the emanations wafting in from the other two cups.

To come to Rabi first: he is no longer the same boy— the sojourn in England has changed him. He has become sexually aware and erotically energized. Keeping a lid on his feelings for his sister-in-law, preventing them from reaching his awareness, has become much more difficult as the waves of sexuality crash against the dykes of morality, throwing his psyche in turmoil. One of the poems in *Chhobi O Gaan*, also dedicated to Kadambari, is 'Rahur Prem' (Rahu's Love). Rahu is a demon of Hindu mythology, a bodiless planet perpetually pursuing a hotly desired moon and occasionally succeeding in swallowing it, resulting in a lunar eclipse.

I hear I do not please you:
Let it be.
Like rugged iron ankle-bands
I'll clasp your feet with grappling hands
Eternally.
A wretched captive in my thrall,
I've seized you,
Fettered your life in my life's chains:
Who'll free you?

Wherever you walk in this world,
Wherever sit, wherever stand,

In spring or winter, day or night,
You'll bear the ceaseless clanking weight
Of this hard heart in shackles round your feet.

. . .

The litany of my name I'll chant with endless weary note,
Like a thorn I'll lie embedded in your foot.
Like a curse from your last life I'll stalk you,
Or doom of your next birth.
Broaching the darkness of my state,
A gloomy night I will create
Your being to engird.
Like two spectres standing side by side,
We two creatures alone will face that endless night.

. . .

In the blank desert of the night
My soul has lost its guiding light:
Eternal thirst, eternal hunger howls.
Now that I have you, how can I
Let go of this perpetual night?
Will any age this monstrous drought allay?
Like a knife in the heart,
Or poison's smart,
Like a plague, like a grief, eternally I'll stay.[4]

There is no tenderness or adoration-from-afar in these verses. They are charged with an unheeding desire for sexual possession. They bespeak of the famished craving for erotic union and the savagery that is unleashed when it is denied. Voracious hungers, violent in their intensity, lurk under the cloak of their refined intimacy. An older Tagore was to write of this period that 'desire was not to be satisfied with mere music, he now wished to savour her physical beauty.'[5]

Jyotirindra, temperamentally inclined to glide over the surface of life, is perhaps oblivious to the sexual undercurrents in the 'silvery peace' of their days of music and song. Or at least that is how Rabindranath perceives him when he comes to write the autobiographical novel *Nashtanir* (The Broken Home), that has the real-life triangle of his youth as its theme. Jyotirindra's worries were of a more pecuniary nature, affecting his self-esteem more than his heart. A business venture that he had embarked upon in a rush of misplaced patriotism—a shipping company to ply steamers on the Ganges in competition with an established British enterprise—failed, leaving him bankrupt. The failure, Rabi felt, was not only because of Jyotirindra's uncalculating and unbusinesslike spirit but also because of his trusting nature of which others took advantage. To escape the knowing and pitying looks of the family—if not any outright recriminations—Jyotirindra spent more and more time away from home at the theatres of Calcutta, trying to forget his troubles in a milieu that shared his real passion.

Of the three, Kadambari has drawn the worst lot. She could have perhaps borne sexual privation as long as she was sure of having Rabi all to herself as in the earlier years of their intimacy. She has been the midwife to his literary career, has quickened Rabi's mind, enlivened his soul, as he has hers. But now there are others in the outside world that lay claim to him and she senses that, often enough, he is quite happy to opt out of their two-person universe. The couple of poems he wrote when she and Jyotirindra were away on a long journey are utterly different from the earlier poems she had loved, although she would never praise them or him to his face.

Thus left in communion with myself alone [in Kadambari's absence] I know not how I slipped out of the poetical groove into which I had fallen. Perhaps being cut off from those who I sought to please and whose taste in poetry moulded the form I tried to

put my thoughts into, I naturally gained freedom. . .'At last,' said
my heart, 'what I write is my own!'[6]

Since his voyage to England, Rabi has discovered that he is
attractive to women, and is attracted by them. Even though he
is back in Jorasanko, he spends much of his time at the central
Calcutta house of his sister-in-law Jnanadanandini, the wife of
his brother Satyendranath with whom he had stayed in England.
Rabi admires her greatly. Unlike the visitors to Jorasanko, people
who meet at the sister-in-law's house have been to England. They
are modern in outlook and Rabi's enjoyment of their company is
evident. Kadambari's husband, too, is away most evenings, either at
Jnanadanandini's place or at the theatre; there are rumours of his
dalliance with actresses, especially a certain Binodini. Kadambari
continues to be childless, a state that is contemptuously attributed to
her barrenness and regarded at best with condescension, especially by
the women. In India of the time, to be barren was a stigma that was
impossible to erase by any number of a woman's accomplishments.
Without motherhood, Kadambari's beautiful singing voice, her
talent for acting and love of literature are worthless. What a fate to
befall a woman who loved children, who brought up her sister-in-law
Swarankumari's youngest daughter Urmila as her own, only to lose
her when the child tripped and fell down the stairs and died. The girl
was only five and had just started school.

As often happens in such situations, the link in the chain under
the greatest strain and with the least possibility of giving vent to
it, snapped. This was Kadambari. Jyoytindra was protected both
by his good-natured insensitivity and the pleasure he found in his
beloved theatre and the company of actresses. Rabi's solace and
redemption lay in the surges of inspiration that were creating the
poems of *Evening Songs*. In poetry he could manifest his pain, 'a cry
more akin to an inarticulate wail than to words of precise meaning',

while connecting to and deriving strength from his core identity as
a poet.

> The sadness and pain which sought expression in Evening Songs
> had their roots in the depths of my being. As one's sleep-smothered
> consciousness wrestles with a nightmare in its efforts to awake,
> so the submerged inner self struggles to free itself from its
> complexities and come out into the open. These Songs are the
> history of that struggle.[7]

There is an uncorroborated report by a Bengali biographer, Prabhat
Mukhopadhaya, who knew Rabindranath, that in early 1882
Kadambari attempted suicide.[8] Rabi's poem 'Tarokar Atmohatya'
(The Suicide of the Star), published in *Bharati* in July 1882, could be
referring to this event, if it ever took place. Or, with his sensitivity
towards Kadambari's inner life and a poet's prescience, he could be
warning of the danger looming ahead. In the poem, searching for
the reason of the star 'whom anguish of mind has driven to suicide /
and the eternal extinction of light,' Rabi asks:

> O what could have befallen?
> No one asked even once
> Why he should have fallen.
>
> Had someone sought to learn,
> I know what answer he would have returned—
> Each day of life, what made him burn.
> The pain of laughter was the grief he bore:
>   That, and nothing more.
> A glowing coal, its gloomy heart to hide,
> Laughs on and on:
>   The more it laughs, the more it burns.

He ends the poem with a wished for Liebestod, lovers choosing to die together, a beloved trope of romantic poetry all over the world, from Romeo and Juliet to Layla and Majnun.

> My heart, my heart, O do you long
> By this dead star in sleep to lie
>   In that sea of darkness,
>   The depths of this night,
>   That fathomless sky?[9]

Rabindranath's answer to the cause of suicide in the poem ignores Jyotindra's and his own contribution to Kadambari's anguish and seems to lay the blame on the conservative women (and men) of the extended family who deride Kadambari's barrenness and ridicule her passion for poems and novels, activities considered highly unsuitable for a respectable woman.

It was in a state of creative exaltation, sexual torment and being a helpless bystander of a dearly loved person's suffering, that Rabi had two visions. The first was while he was pacing the terrace of the Jorasanko house at sunset when he felt the twilight 'lifting the cover of triviality from the everyday world'; even the walls of adjoining houses grew beautiful.

> I could see at once that it was the effect of the evening which had come within me; its shades had obliterated my self. While the self was rampant during the glare of day, everything I perceived was mingled with and hidden by it. Now, that the self was put into the background, I could see the world in its own true aspect. And that aspect has nothing of triviality in it, it is full of beauty and joy.[10]

The other vision, while staying with Jyotirindra and Kadambari in their Calcutta house in Sudder Street, was more lasting in its after-

effects. He was standing on the verandah of the house early in the
morning looking at the sun rising through the leafy treetops.

> As I continued to gaze, all of a sudden a covering seemed to fall
> away from my eyes, and I found the whole world bathed in a
> wonderful radiance, with waves of beauty and joy swelling on
> every side. This radiance pierced in a moment through the folds
> of sadness and despondency which had accumulated over my
> heart, and flooded it with universal light.
>
> That very day the poem The Awakening of the Waterfall
> [Nirjharer Swapnabhanga] gushed forth and coursed on like a
> veritable cascade.[11]

How have the sun's rays in my heart
Entered this morning! How have the songs
Of morning birds into the dark cave broken!
Who knows why, after long, my soul has woken!
The soul awakes, the waters stir:
I cannot stem my heart's passion, my heart's desire.

    The earth shudders and quakes
    And massive rocks roll down,
    The swollen foaming flood
    Rages with furious groans:
    It rushes here, it rushes there,
    Whirling in a madman's gyre—
Seeks to break out, but cannot see where lies the prison door.
    Why is God so stony-hearted?
    Why with his bonds am I begirded?
    Break them, my heart, break every stay—
    Work the will for life today,
Summon wave upon wave, blow upon blow.

When the soul is roused to gladness,

What are rocks, and what is darkness?

What need I fear, when longing surges so?

I'll pour out my compassion:

I'll burst this rocky dungeon,

I'll break in flood, I'll comb the world with my distracted song;

Gathering flowers with hair untied,

My rainbow-coloured wings spread wide,

Laughing among the sun's bright beams, pour out my soul in pleasure.

From crag to crag I'll swiftly race,

Plunging along the mountain face,

With laughter swell, with music flow, and clap hands to measure.

So much of words, so much of song, so much of life have I,

So much delight, so much desire—a heart in ecstasy.

What can it mean? My soul today has woken after long—

I seem to hear from far away the mighty ocean's song.

On every side

What prison walls abide—

O break the walls, rain blow on blow, break free:

What song the birds have sung today, what sunshine do I see.[12]

Throughout his life, Rabindranath considered 'Nirjharer Swapnabhanga' vital for his development as a poet, a prelude to all his future poetry.[13]

Once again we see that, as with his father Debendranath and other spiritually gifted young persons throughout the world, the psyche when exceptionally agitated, in extremis, does not always collapse into a state of pathological deformation but can open up to extraordinary psychic, 'mystical' experiences. Rabi's visions arose from the activation of an intense, connective imagination, a consciousness to which mystics, writers and artists through the ages have borne witness. The consciousness that gives birth to connective imagination refuses to fit into the current scientific paradigm of mind and consciousness being inseparable from their biological substratum, a paradigm that does not admit the possibility of a mind that is not only biological but also has a transcendental dimension.

For me, 'Nirjharer Swapnabhanga' connects the biological with the transcendent. If the sun is the symbol of the spirit and the sea that of our biological unconscious depths, then the waterfall in the poem is the connecting link between the two. Rabindranath senses this connection when, commenting on the poem in *The Religion of Man*, he says, 'The waterfall, whose spirit lay dormant in its ice bound isolation, was touched by the sun and, bursting in a cataract of freedom, it found its finality in an unending sacrifice, in a continual union with the sea.'[14] Like many of his other, later poems, 'Nirjharer Swapnabhanga' is not purely 'spiritual' but connects yearnings of the spirit with desires of the body. We do Rabindranath injustice when we highlight only the mystic in the poet and discount the sensualist.

In the outer world, events are picking up pace. Rabi's marriage is being arranged. In early September 1883, his father summons him to Dalhousie. Within three weeks of his return to Calcutta, the choice falls on Bhabatarini (after marriage, her old-fashioned name was changed to Mrinalini), a ten-year-old girl, neither good-looking nor literate, the daughter of a Pirali Brahmin working on the Tagore estates near Jessore in eastern Bengal. On 9 December, the wedding takes place in a simple ceremony at the Jorasanko house. Rabi 'had sent out a few cards to his friends in which he wrote that "his intimate relative Rabindranath Tagore is to be married"—implying that the real Rabindranath was detached from the event', write Dutta and Robinson.[15] Maybe he was also embarrassed, they add in parentheses. As he well might be, remembering his passionately held views on the importance of intellectual curiosity and social adeptness in a wife

in his letters from England. Given his strongly stated opposition to
the then prevalent custom of child marriage, there must also have
been self-recriminations in marrying a ten-year-old girl. In a poem
published in the collection *Manashi*, 'The Lady of the Mind', in 1890,
dedicated once again to Kadambari, the self-recrimination shades
into self-loathing.

> Playing our flutes, let us bring home a bride of eight years. Let
> us snatch and tear open the bud of childhood, let us force out the
> sweet youth! Pressing a weight of scriptures on the new expanding
> life, let us make it one with the dust of the wrinkled ages![16]

In both of Rabindranath's autobiographical writings, there is not a
single mention of his wife. For someone whose 'memory pictures'
are drawn in such vivid detail, the marriage is dismissed in two terse
sentences—'Shortly after my return from Karwar, I was married. I
was then 22 years of age.'[17]

An eyewitness account of the wedding tells us that instead of
filling up the small clay pots in a traditional ritual, Rabi started
turning them upside down. On being chided by one of his aunts he
replied that since everything had turned topsy-turvy, he was doing
the same with the clay pots. Requested by the aunt to sing, he looked
at his veiled wife, who he had not met before and who was reputed
to be plain-looking, and began 'O my beautiful one!'[18] For more
than a year he lived separately from his child-bride who was sent to
stay with Jnanadanandini so that she could be educated and learn
the ways of the modern Anglo-Bengali world.

On 19 April 1884, four months after Rabi's marriage, Kadambari
swallowed opium she had secretly procured and died two days later.
To avoid scandal, the coroner's report, along with a rumoured letter
explaining the reasons for her suicide, as well as all her other letters,
were destroyed on orders of Debendranath. In the family account

book, there is an entry, 'Expenses towards suppressing the news of the death to the press Rs 52.'

As we saw above, Kadambari's dysphoric tendency had started to become dangerously heightened as she felt that Rabi had begun to move away from her. His marriage was then only a final blow in a cumulative trauma that had been some time in the making. For this sensitive and, by some accounts, highly strung woman, the marriage marked an end to her emotional life, in whose permanent absence the biological one was not worth living. I would also speculate that the sorrow of her childlessness had been cushioned by her being a mother to Rabi after Sharada Devi's death, seeing to his 'food and clothing and all other wants'. Rabi had not only been an intimate companion but, in her unconscious fantasy, also a lover—and son. His marriage destroyed the fantasy's consolatory power, exposed Kadambari to the shattering reality that there would never be a child for her, no direct substitute for Rabi.

Sixteen years later, Rabindranath would look back at the three protagonists of the triangle in his story, *Nashtanir* (The Broken Home), published in 1901. Bhupati, a wealthy young man, is married to a child-bride Charulata who grows into a comely young woman without the husband registering the change in his wife. Bhupati spends most of his time outside home, totally involved in his venture of running a newspaper. He occasionally suffers pangs of guilt at neglecting his young wife and feels that because of the lack of female company, Charulata must be lonely at home. He asks his brother-in-law Umapati and his wife Mandakini to come and live with them so that Charulata is not on her own.

Charulata likes to read and develops a close relationship with Bhupati's cousin Amal who lives in the same house and is a college student. Amal likes to make demands on Charulata: hand-knitted carpet slippers, specially cooked meals. There are times when Charu makes mock protests 'but the truth was that she was in desperate need of someone who in turn needed her, depended on her, and whom she could spoil affectionately'.[19] Amal has literary ambitions and Charu encourages him to write and to read out to her what he has written. And Amal would do just that, even if it was an incomplete composition that he had just begun writing. The two of them would be utterly absorbed in discussing how the rest of that essay could be completed. So deep was this immersion in literature that all else would be pushed to the background.

Amal's first essay is published and he even gets a few appreciative letters from admirers, some of them female. Charu discovers that she is not as pleased as she ought to be at this turn of events. She feels that Amal's writings belong to an intimate realm that he should share only with her. Now the privacy they enjoyed together had been shattered, opening the floodgates for others to encroach upon their private realm. One of these intruders is the sister-in-law, Manda, who had been earlier indifferent to Amal but now, with the rise in his status, often invites Amal to read to her, upsetting Charu even more.

Charu insinuates to Bhupati that Amal is paying the sister-in-law undue attention, but Bhupati, who is preoccupied with the looming bankruptcy of his paper, dismisses the complaint with a light-hearted remark. Bhupati's financial problems are due to his lack of business sense and his trusting nature, which has been betrayed by Manda's husband who has cheated him. Amal believes that the couple had to leave because of Charu's allegation that there was something improper in his relationship with Manda and ignores Charu. She tries to win him back by writing a piece herself and attempting to share it with him but Amal evinces no interest. Bhupati receives a proposal for Amal's marriage from a lawyer who is also willing to send Amal to England after the marriage. Amal readily agrees to the proposal. In her pain, Charu is sarcastic, blaming Amal for hiding his own wish to be married, which she likens to a 'ravenous hunger'. Trying to make light of the situation, Bhupati jokes that Amal perhaps kept this 'hunger' hidden because Charulata might become jealous of his wife. Stung by this, Charulata rebukes Bhupati for making such a careless, unthinking remark.

After Amal's marriage and departure for England, Charu has a gradual breakdown. Tormented by memories of Amal, she retreats into her room in great distress. She repeats Amal's name to herself and speaks to him as if he was present, cursing herself for not having parted from him more amicably and declaring that she can never forget him. In her grief, she even hears Amal responding to her plaintive pleas from across the seas. Nothing seems to assuage her anguish and anxiety. Even an otherwise unobservant Bhupati notices that his wife looks morose and preoccupied. He makes an effort to come closer to her by writing a literary piece himself which he wants to show Charu, but meets with her indifference. Amal's absence continues to gnaw at Charu. Even the mention of his name would make her tense, and she would often abruptly leave a conversation to weep copiously. None of this escapes Bhupati, and the rude realization of it all wrecks his world. He decides to start another newspaper in far-off Mysore. As he is leaving, Charu asks him to take her with him. Bhupati feels Charu wants to go with him only because she cannot bear to live in the house that is filled with Amal's memories and the agony of her separation from him. He refuses.

> Drained of blood Charu's face turned white. She firmly gripped the bed with both her hands for support. Looking at Charu, Bhupati immediately changed his mind. 'Well Charu, come with me then,' he told Charu
>
> 'No, let it be,' responded Charu.[20]

In these last lines of the novella it is apparent that the unwritten final act of the drama can only end in Charu's suicide.

Rabindranath seems to attribute Charulata's depression to the intrusion of the world into the hothouse of their intimacy, the shattering of a private, enchanted sphere, followed by her feeling of being abandoned by Amal. Their relationship had given Charu life; its end took that life away. He absolves Bhupati of having played any role in the tragedy except as an innocent bystander. Like Jyotirindra, Bhupati is an amiable man, without much interest in the complexities of human emotion, which he senses but inarticulately in his wife. Baffled by her moods, his clumsy efforts to come close to her spurned, he may at the most be accused of a lack of empathy, not neglect.

In *Nashtanir*, Rabindranath is silent on the effect that the ending of the relationship, and Charu's depression, had on Amal. In real life, three years after her death, continuing the theme of 'The Suicide of a Star', Rabi rails against a cruel world (the extended Tagore family?) that drove her to suicide and who would now erase her memory.

> What joy is there on earth for those who are noble, with a heart capable of great affection? None at all. They are like the veena whose every string vibrates when smitten by the cruelties of the world. The music thus produced captivates everyone—but no one sighs at the thought of this pain appearing in the garb of music. . .The veena is smitten by all and sundry—most of them cruel and heartless who do not care to remember her. They do not consider this veena as God's blessing. Considering themselves to be masters, they often tread upon the manifestation of all that is gentle, sweet and pure in a fit of disdain or indifference![21]

Later, in his *Reminiscences*, Rabindranath gives full vent to the devastation that Kadambari's suicide produced in his own inner world.

> When, of a sudden, death came, and in a moment tore a gaping rent in its [life's] smooth-seeming fabric, I was utterly bewildered.

All around, the trees, the soil, the water, the sun, the moon, the stars, remained as immovably true as before; and yet the person who was as truly there, who, through a thousand points of contact with life, mind and heart, was ever so much more true for me, had vanished in a moment like a dream. What perplexing self-contradiction it all seemed to me as I looked around! How was I ever to reconcile what remained with which had gone?

The terrible darkness which was disclosed to me through this rent, continued to attract me night and day as time went on. I would ever and anon return to take my stand there and gaze upon it, wondering what there was left in place of what had gone.[22]

Alone on the terrace at night, groping like a 'blind man trying to find some device or sign upon the black stone of death', Rabi tried to find meaning in a death that had emptied his universe. What lightened his mind was his association of death with freedom. Death frees one from slavery to the reality principle, from the prison of 'stony-hearted facts'. It compensates for the all-pervading pressure of worldly existence and thus 'The terrible weight of an unopposed life force has not to be endured by man—this truth came over me that day as a sudden, wonderful revelation.'[23]

In his outer behaviour, in what he calls 'a recrudescence of eccentricity', he discarded all conventions of dress as he wandered into fashionable bookshops wrapped in a coarse sheet and with his feet shod in a pair of slippers. In all kinds of weather, hot or cold, he slept out on the veranda of the third storey, next to the terrace, where 'the stars and I could gaze at each other, and no time was lost in greeting the dawn'.[24]

In searching for something where nothing is visible, some may discern in Rabi's efforts to cope with the trauma of Kadambari's death the erection of a defensive wall against a massive onrush of emotions threatening a mental breakdown. One of these emotions,

I believe, is a repressed feeling of guilt. I base this speculation not only on my reading of his poems about Kadambari but also my impressions from clinical practice among the Indian middle and upper middle classes, where often a close, intimate relationship develops between the younger brother and the wife of an elder brother, especially if the difference in their ages is small and the wife feels neglected by the husband. I have found that women who are on terms of intimacy with a younger brother-in-law experience a strong depressive anxiety that is occasioned by his leaving home or his impending marriage, which the woman perceives as an end to her emotional life. And if this is followed up with a clinical depression or even an attempted suicide, there is little that the brother-in-law can do to avoid conscious or unconscious pangs of guilt.

Kadambari's tragic death cast a shadow on Rabindranath's psyche that would endure through the rest of his life. The mourning of Kadambari's absence and the summoning of her presence keep recurring in Rabindranath's poems, songs, fiction and later, in old age, also in his paintings. Gradually assimilated into his psyche and irradiating large parts of his ouevre, the work of mourning, which is not about forgetting but about remembering, lent his creativity that certain depth which distinguishes the genius from the merely talented. We must also remember that keeping the memory of Kadambari alive in mourning was also to tap into the passion of his youthful love, with love's power to heighten his literary and artistic creativity. We know that the exultation of passionate love deepens the lover's sensate and metaphysical responsiveness, enhances his creativity at the same time that it lends strength to a self that may have been otherwise debilitated by the creative process.

In his life, though, the shadow would make the pit of depression into which he sometimes fell darker and deeper. To take one example, the severest depression of all when he was fifty-three years old lasted for almost a year. His friend C.F. Andrews—to whom he wrote almost every day at the onset of depression, and when he was recovering from it—felt that the mental suffering was due to the poet's sensing of the impeding catastrophe of the First World War. Other biographers have attributed it to his feelings of failure in meeting the various demands made on him— the management of the Tagore estates, the dire financial situation of the Shantiniketan school, the political anti-British ferment in the country from which he was holding aloof and, in consequence, was being criticized by many as a lackey of British imperialism.

To these, Rabindranath added the effects of a Unani medicine he had been taking. In a long letter he wrote to his son Rathindranath during a short period of respite, Rabindranath describes his own state:

> Day and night I am haunted with ideas of death and wanting to die. Feels like I have not been able to do anything ever, and will not be able to do anything in future, my life is altogether a waste; mistrust and irritation about all others around me. While in Ramgarh my *'conscience'* has been hammering most terribly that I have not carried out any of my responsibilities towards my university, zamindari, family, country. . .I am usually so dispassionate and peaceful by nature that I can't imagine how something like this can happen to me. These days I seem to be going in some complete opposite direction to my usual nature—the way I am clinging onto all of you, day and night, is quite unfair and ridiculous. For that I only have disrespect towards myself. . .I was *'deliberately'* committing *'suicide'*—there was not an iota of satisfaction in my life. Whatever I was touching I was throwing it all over. How one can be such a completely opposite kind of a person is a new 'experience' for me—all like a dense net of nightmares.[25]

In his novel *Ghare Baire* (The Home and the World)—which Rabindranath was writing during this period of emotional vulnerability before it collapsed into a breakdown in which no creative work was possible—Nikhil the landowner, who is Rabindranath's fictional mask, begins his story by agonizing over the depressive state in which he finds himself.

> There is a thorn somewhere pricking in my heart, constantly giving me pain while I am about my daily work. It seems to persist even when I am asleep. The very moment I wake up in the morning, I find that the bloom has gone from the face of the sky. What is it? What has happened?
>
> My mind has become so sensitive, that even my past life, which came to me in the disguise of happiness, seems to wring my very heart with its falsehood; and the shame and sorrow which are coming close to me are losing their cover of privacy, all the more because they try to veil their faces. My heart has become all eyes. The things that should not be seen, the things I do not want to see—these I must see. . .And I am unworthy, unworthy, unworthy.[26]

Rabindranath is aware of the impending depression in his letters to Andrews though in the beginning he seeks to understand it as a spiritual crisis. The letters employ spiritual language to describe his suffering, consciously or unconsciously echoing the depictions of many mystics of their 'dark night of the soul':

> I am struggling on my way through the wilderness. The light from across the summit is clear; but the shadows are bleeding and deep on the slope of the dark valley. My feet are bleeding, and I am toiling with panting breath. Wearied, I lie down upon the dust and cry and call upon His name.[27]

By 25 May, he believes the phase is over as 'Morning has dawned upon me at last. My wrestling with the shadows is over.'[28] What returns in

July 1914 to last, with intermittent periods of respite, till February of next year is unequivocally a clinical depression and recognized as such by Rabindranath himself, and others around him. 'I feel I am on the verge of a breakdown. Therefore I must take flight to the solitude of the Padma. I need rest and the nursing of Nature,' he writes in one letter,[29] and, recovering, 'You are right. I had been suffering from a time of deep depression and weariness.'[30]

My own take on Rabindranath's depressive episode is through a psychoanalytic lens. The clouds, I would say, had already begun to gather when he returned from England where he was feted and lionized. It is noteworthy that the depression begins in May 1914, less than six months after he learns in November 1913 that he has been awarded the Nobel Prize for Literature: 'I have scaled the peak and found no shelter in fame's bleak and barren height.'[31] In other words, when the outer world is testifying to Rabindranath's worth, the inner one is telling him that he is worthless. This is not unusual, given that along with fame comes an end to privacy, a horror for such a private person as Rabindranath. Fame also makes one vulnerable to envy, criticism and attack. The sensitive person may also have intimations of 'separation guilt', the pre-eminent form of guilt in the Indian setting. With its strong 'relational orientation', as contrasted with a more individualistic orientation of north European and American cultures, the Indian family tends to foster the unconscious belief that a person is disloyal to his loved ones if he moves too far ahead of them, that success on such a scale will isolate the person, cut off his ties to others, as also to his own childhood identity.[32]

In a psyche debilitated by the losses of his father, wife and two children in the preceding decade, Rabindranath's depression began, I would say, with highly charged memories of the dead who Rabi had loved and who had loved Rabi as a child and youth—with Kadambari in their forefront—forcing a way into his consciousness. On coming across a picture of Kadambari, sometime in 1914, Rabindranath had

written a poem, 'Tumi ki keboli chobi?'' (Are you a mere picture?).
In it, he mournfully contrasts the stillness of her picture in the frame
with the life that had once animated every limb of her body, with
her verve that had gushed out into song and dance that resonated
with the rhythm of the universe. But then,

> While walking this path together
> You suddenly stopped behind darkness
> After that I have trodden alone day-and-night,
> Looking ahead, facing much in life.
> You have stopped in the middle of the road,
> You stand still there.
> Hiding behind the grass, the dust, the stars, the sun, the moon,
> Behind all of them, you are just a picture.

And yet as someone who pervades every particle of Rabindranath's
universe, '. . .the poet inside the poet/ 'You are not, you cannot be,
a picture.'[33]

In *Ghare Baire*, written in the same period, Nikhil's nostalgic
recollection of childhood scenes with his sister-in-law are clearly
Rabindranath's own memories of Kadambari.

> We have played together, through the drowsy afternoons, in a
> corner of the roof terrace. I have thrown down to her green
> amras from the tree-top to be made into deliciously indigestible
> chutnies by slicing them up with mustard, salt and fragrant herbs.
> It was my part to gather for her all the forbidden things from the
> store-room to be used in the marriage celebration of her dolls. .
> .And then, as we grew up, our mutual joys and sorrows took on
> deeper tones of intimacy.[34]

The beginning of Rabindranath's depression also coincides with an

'anniversary reaction', the bringing up of distressing memories on
the birth or death anniversary of a loved person who might have
died long ago but where the loss feels as if it happened recently. The
person here is Rabindranath's father, Debendranath. In his letter of
17 May to Andrews, we read.

> Today is my father's birthday anniversary. We have just had our
> morning prayer, and my mind is full. . .I have been experiencing
> the feeling of great expectation, although it has also its elements
> of great suffering. To be born naked in the heart of the eternal
> Truth; to be able to feel with my entire being the life-throb of
> the universal heart—that is the cry of my soul. I tell you all this,
> so that you may understand what I am passing through and may
> help me when the occasion arrives.[35]

Rabindranath's own diagnosis of the depression is a depletion of
the 'subconscious nature [which] must have sufficient time to store
up what our conscious nature requires'.[36] This is uncanny echoing
of what a psychoanalyst, too, would say about his depression. The
depletion, the emptying of Rabindranath's self in depression, I
would conjecture, has to do with the unconscious mental images
of the loved persons of childhood who constituted a vital part of
Rabindranath's self now becoming bereft of vitality. The images have
become lifeless, lost their power to sustain the self. The memories
of Kadambari and his father that now hold sway are not merely of
loss, of a 'sweet sorrow' that a poet may even welcome at times. The
memories have acquired menacing visages that otherwise lie interred
in the vault of the repressed unconscious but have now emerged to
threaten the stability of the self. The unconscious or preconscious
memories of their love—of mother, father, Kadambari—have
paled. In their most elementary form, ignoring all the nuances and
complexities which we can never know, these memories are imbued

with anger and grief at being abandoned by the mother, resentment of the overbearing father, guilt at having betrayed Kadambari and feeling responsible for her death. They are the 'shame and sorrow' of which Nikhil speaks in *Ghare Baire*, or 'the unsuspected accumulations of untruth and self-deception' in 'the hidden corners of my being' of which Rabindranath writes in a letter to Andrews.[37]

Rabindranath's cure for his depression was an old one from his childhood: solitude, preferably in the 'silvery peace' of his beloved Padma.

> Directly I came to myself and I am healed. The cure for all the illnesses of life is stored at the inner depth of life itself, the access to which becomes possible when we are alone. This solitude is a world in itself full of wonders and resources unthought-of. It is so absurdly near you yet so unapproachably distant. But I do not want to talk. Please forgive my absence and silence. I cannot afford to scatter my mind away just now—these moments are solemn to me.[38]

To the terrace and the inner garden of his childhood, he had added another site, this one from his youth: the Padma. Each of them was an insulated sanctuary, or what the psychoanalyst William Niederland would call 'a walled-off garden away not only from the turbulence and strife of the outer world but also from irksome emotional problems and involvement with people. It is under such circumstances that, in the gifted person, the world of repressed visual, auditory, and kinesthetic memories emerges, which the artist transmutes into the creative act.'[39] These three sites were Rabindranath's personal symbols of both curative and also creative power. He would return to them frequently, physically or in imagination, especially in times of psychic turmoil, and emerge strengthened.

10

Art and Psyche: The Paintings

I feel somewhat presumptuous in writing of Rabindranath's paintings when I have no expertise in matters relating to art. Along with many others, I truly believe that there is an ultimate mystery at the heart of great art, a beauty that can all too easily vanish if we seek to understand it too easily and too quickly.[1] I am also cautioned by the painter himself who wrote of his paintings: 'People often ask me about the meaning of my pictures. I remain silent even as my pictures are. It is for them to express and not to explain.'[2] And at another place: 'I have nothing to say about my pictures. I do not really know what I have done, or wanted to say.'[3] It would thus be presumptuous of me to try and explain Rabindranath's pictures in any authoritative fashion. As with his poems and other writings, all I can do here is to try and capture a glimpse of the mysterious creativity of his paintings through the impressions they have left on my own mind. In other words, it is not any scholarly apparatus but my own psyche which is the primary source of my observations, my own unconscious with which I seek to understand the unconscious in Rabindranath's paintings, predominantly the landscapes and the female portraits. I thus promise to be hopelessly subjective as I attempt an answer to the question the surrealist Andre Breton asked in a different context: 'To me a picture is a window that looks out on something, the question is—on what?' What do Rabindranath's paintings, then, look out on?

Given his reputation—based on his literary output, especially his poems and songs—of being a highly 'spiritual' person, it would be easy to claim that the creativity Rabindranath displays in his art is fundamentally spiritual.[4] This will not be erroneous, certainly as far as some of his landscapes are concerned.

These landscapes are indeed like many of his poems: contemplative, simultaneously looking in and looking out. They recapture young Rabindranath's moments of quasi-mystical absorption in nature, such as when he writes in a letter of the '. . .shining expanse of river, the blur of shade thrown by the dark fringe of trees along its edge, and the white sky gleaming overhead in uncontrolled aloofness'.[5] I believe it is significant that when in September 1937, Rabindranath was in a coma for sixty hours and almost died, his first creative act

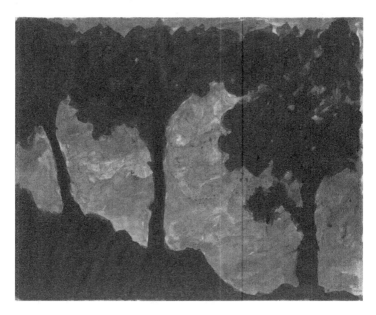

on coming back from the borderland between life and death, was to ask for colours and a brush, and, propped up on pillows, paint a landscape on a piece of plywood, 'dark trees outlined against a ghostly twilight beneath which glimmered irregular patches of white light with the hint of palest yellow'.[6]

His landscapes, in which Tagore seems to try to recapture 'my blood tie with the earth, my kinsman's love for her', the painter is gazing into nature with such an empathy that he seems to be connecting with the universe itself. The rows of trees and the masses of dark clouds that are recurrent motifs in his landscapes go back to his boyhood when he returned home in the afternoons from a hated school and as soon as he got down from the carriage 'looked up at the eastern sky above the third-storey roof, to see dark blue clouds in a thickened dense mass. In a moment a sense of wonder denser than the clouds would amass in my mind. On one side lay the distant sky softened by clouds, on the other a boy's heart thrilled with wonder. . .'[7]

Yet, excluding some of the landscapes, my abiding impression of the bulk of Rabindranath's paintings is that their spirituality lies more

in their *execution* than in their *inspiration*. If, in Coomaraswamy's terms, artistic creativity is a two-step yoga comprising, one, a meditative stance, mindfulness, and two, skilled execution,[8] then the yoga of Rabindranath's paintings lies more in their execution. The painter himself recognizes this particularity when he writes in a letter to Rani Mahalanobis:

> The subject matter of a poem can be traced back to some dim
> thought in the mind. . .While painting, the process adopted by
> me is quite the reverse. First, there is the hint of a line, then the

line becomes a form. The more pronounced the form the clearer becomes the picture of my conception. This creation of form is an endless wonder.[9]

The spiritual aspect of Rabindranath's art, especially in the landscapes, is thus not that of a meditating monk but the arrow-maker who is often brought up in Indian philosophical texts as the proverbial instance of mindfulness. Thus, Shankaracharya (seventh century AD), one of the greatest Indian philosophers singles out '. . . the arrow-maker [who] perceives nothing beyond his work when he is buried in it'.[10]

For a psychoanalyst, though, Rabindranath's paintings are also shapes of his unconscious feelings arising from his early relationships which he recaptures and transforms in the present through his art.

This psychoanalytic approach to understanding art has limitations because of the wide variety in works of art. It works best with artists like Eduard Munch and Pablo Picasso (and in our country, M.F. Husain and F.N. Souza, for instance) who have poured their personal lives into their work and offer abundant material for responsible psychoanalytic exploration. I count Rabindranath among this group. The approach will not easily work in the case of artists who work in a tradition that emphasizes faithfulness to a well-defined iconography and technique. These artists subordinate the personal in the service of an aesthetic or a religious ideal and the personal unconscious, though present in the art work, will be difficult to detect.[11] In other words, this approach works best with modern art that has placed the individual subjectivity of the artist at the centre of aesthetic experience and creative process, as had Rabindranath. But even in modern art, it will be difficult, though not impossible, to detect unconscious biographical themes in the work of many modern painters where the narrative content of the painting, its subject, is completely subordinated to its purely visual or formal elements: the arrangement of its lines, shapes, and colours. Of course, it is this visual music, the *emotion of form*,[12] which turns the *emotion of content* in a painting into a work of art. But if this formal, abstract music is overpoweringly loud, it becomes difficult to hear the major unconscious themes of the artist's life story. Rabindranath, who has been called the 'father of Indian modernism' in painting, is a modernist precisely because he recognizes that his paintings are animated by the music of form, which he calls rhythm, form being the last elaboration of meaning.

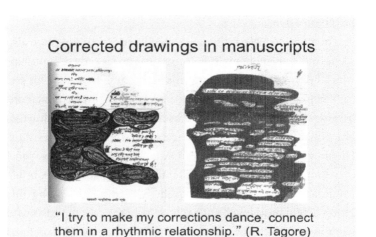

Corrected drawings in manuscripts

"I try to make my corrections dance, connect them in a rhythmic relationship." (R. Tagore)

As he says:

One thing which is common to all arts is the principle of rhythm which transforms inert materials into living creations. My instinct for it and my training in its use led me to know that lines and colours in art are no carriers of information; they seek their rhythmic incarnation in pictures.[13]

Regarding his corrective drawings in his manuscript, he writes: 'I try to make my corrections dance, connect them in a rhythmic relationship and transform accumulation into adornment.'[14] And at another place '. . .in my case my pictures did not have their origin in trained discipline, in tradition and deliberate attempt at illustration, but in my instinct for rhythm, my pleasure in harmonious combination of lines and colours'.[15]

Yet, Rabindranath's paintings, especially his portraits, have enough of narrative content to let me recognize some dominant themes of his unconscious inner life, having their origins in his early childhood years which are then repeated again and again during the course of his long life, as they are repeated in all our lives.

As we know, Rabindranath came to painting late, when he was almost seventy years old. The immediate precursor of his paintings were the *Puravi* poems which he wrote during an ocean crossing from Cherbourg to Buenos Aires. During the voyage, we are told, he was violently ill and his mind was 'despondent with the saddest thoughts of the tragedy of love and death'.[16] With a weakening of the normal psychological defences that keep a lid on the cauldron of our unconscious impulses, the cut-off parts of the self bubbled up through many lines in the first drafts of these poems which Rabindranath then erased and formed into shapes he called 'apparitions of non-deliberate origin'. Summoned from a deeply buried vault of memory, I wonder how much similarity they bear to the childhood apparitions that so terrified him when, in the helplessness and loneliness of his exile, Rabi would dare to walk the narrow passage from the outer apartments to the inner quarters at night.

In one poem in *Puravi* he directly refers to these drawings:

Hark, where in the formless limbs, ghosts of sights and weepings haunt the night. . .A time was when they had a form and a voice. . .
The fruitless sorrow of all that has been and is now nameless,

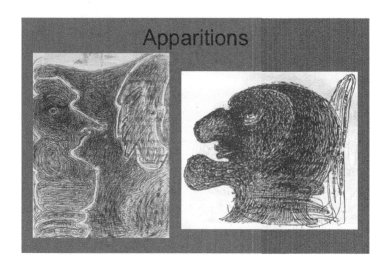

amorphous, unremembered, haunt the dim recesses of my mind seeking a form, a shelter.[17]

Not that he had not earlier used the same technique of erasing lines from poems and transforming the erasures into rhythmic visual shapes. But, as Kshitis Roy perceptively observes, the important difference now is 'that while the earlier erasures mostly assumed delicately floriated or vine-like patterns, the ones of *Puravi* often show an orgy of violent forms—grotesque and primitive shapes— that are almost in conflict with the words and the lines, and, at times very nearly obliterating a whole stanza or a complete poem.'[18] From *Puravi* onwards, under a greater pressure from unconscious promptings, poetry recedes and painting comes more and more to the fore; the poet Tagore cedes his place to the painter Rabindranath. In the same letter to Rani Mahalanobis dated 7 November 1928 from which I quoted earlier, he writes, 'The most important item in the bulletin of my daily news, is my painting. I am hopelessly entangled in the spell that the lines have cast all around me. . .I have almost managed to forget that there used to be a time when I wrote poetry.'[19]

Is painting, the psychoanalyst would ask, potentially more therapeutic than poetry in a situation of extreme emotional turmoil? Do the disturbances caused by the greater play of the unconscious require a stronger medicine? My tentative answer to both questions is, yes. It was in the last stage of his life, old age, that cut-off parts of the self once again demanded a hearing before life came to a close while the unlived or unresolved issues of earlier stages of life again sprang to the fore, bringing the connected emotions of anxiety, guilt and depression in their wake. The wisdom we attribute to the old and believe we see reflected on their faces often masks the cry of an old person's despairing heart.

In an earlier chapter, I have discussed a major theme of Tagore's inner theatre: his urge to bring together and seek harmony among his many dualities—male and female, inside and outside, India–West, human–divine, the works of man and the inspiration of nature—that is also a signal feature of Tagore's literary oeuvre and philosophical writings.

The tension between the dualities in his psyche and his striving to produce harmony among them is also the motor of Tagore's art.[20] Generally, in explanations of artistic creativity, the focus has been on one duality: male and female elements in the artist's psyche, and their integration. Eminent artists of both genders almost universally profess that androgyny is critical to artistic productivity. They assert that 'every artist is androgynous. . .It is the masculine in a woman and the feminine in a man that proves creative' (Sarton), 'the great mind must be androgynous' (Samuel Coleridge), and 'some collaboration has to take place in the mind between woman and man before the act of creation can be accomplished. Some marriage of opposites has to be consummated' (Virginia Woolf).[21] This androgyny is not absent in Tagore's creative output. Indeed, it is a marked feature of his head studies.

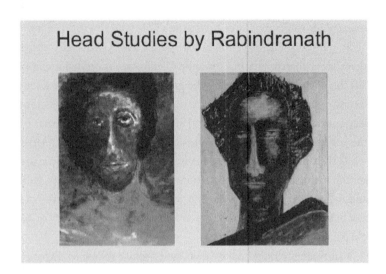

And in the twelve self-portraits he created by coloured doodles on a black and white photograph of himself, one is a woman while the gender of yet another cannot be determined.

The harmony of the masculine and feminine is not only true of his art but also of his person. As Erik Erikson has observed in an unpublished essay on Tagore:

> Some express this (the androgyny) only in their poetry, some in their appearance as well. And Tagore's whole appearance, at the end seemed to be above the sexes, even as in young years, he combined feminine shyness with a tall, masculine body. His beard was patriarchal but his robes veiled some mysteriously pregnant body. Ascetic Gandhi was tolerant of this flamboyant appearance: he understood that it marked Tagore's role in India and the world: for in a country smitten by the necessity to stand up against a conqueror's idol (namely, the masculinity of the British beefeaters) and in a world about to surrender to a combination of technological superman and nationalist bullies, Tagore reasserted

the traditional inclusion in the Indian identity of the feminine and the maternal, the sensual and the experiential, the receptive and the transcendental in human life.[22]

As we saw in an earlier chapter, the duality theme in Tagore's life can be traced back to the 'geography' of his childhood. Here, 'imprisoned' on the *fringe* of the big house with the servants, 'the child Rabi longs for the mysterious *inner sanctum* (his mother's quarters, her 'scent', an immersion in the maternal) as also for the great *outer world*— of the returning father, the inspiration of nature, the merger with the Great Spirit',[23] depicted in his landscapes as the white sky with its 'uncontrolled aloofness'.

The two basic moods of this theme—sadness because the harmony is absent, and rapture when the harmony does take place— are pervasive in Rabindranath's poetry. In his paintings, though, especially in his many female portraits, the predominant mood is of sadness or, I would go even further, of melancholy.

Rabindranath is well aware of the dysphoric mood of these paintings.

> The picture has about it a sense of brooding melancholy—don't you notice it! Most of my pictures are like that—they lack laughter. I do not know why this should be so when I like a good laugh myself and love to make others laugh: Probably I have a touch of sadness—deep down.[24]

Indeed, the sadness was not apparent in his behaviour. As he writes in *Of Myself*:

> Seventy years are over, and even today my friends remonstrate with me upon my levity, and often there is a lapse in my seriousness. . .And after all I cannot afford to waste my days encircled by a moat of seriousness.[25]

He is aware, though, that an artist reveals himself unconsciously
in his creative work and 'that is why I go to poetry and drama for
evidence'.[26]

In their dark colours, profusion of shadows, the expressions on their
half-covered faces, I see not the sadness of loss, the mourning for a
beloved person with whom the relationship was only positive—but,
'deep down', in the unconscious, the melancholy of the loss of a
vitally important relationship that was marked by some *ambivalence*,
where the mourning also has a strain of guilt and perhaps also
bitterness at being abandoned.

Shifting from his paintings to his life, it is no surprise to learn that
the other half of the important relationship was Kadambari. We are
told that, in a conversation with Nandlal Bose, Rabindranath said
that while drawing the female face he is reminded of his sister-in-law
Kadambari Devi. 'The look of the eyes of *natun bouthan* [as he called

her] have become so deeply imprinted on my mind that I can never forget them and when I paint portraits, quite often her glowing eyes present themselves before my sight. Probably that is why the eyes in my portraits take after her eyes.'[27] He had composed a celebrated song in her memory which had the lines *Noyono shomukhe tumi nayi* (You appear not in front of my eyes / Yet you have found a place at the centre of my vision).[28] Haunted by Kadambari's ghostly presence, Rabindranath tried to give her tangibility through his paintings (and poems).

It is important to note that I am not saying that Rabindranath's female portraits are of Kadambari. An artwork does not literally recreate the lost person; it does not effect a direct substitution. What it seeks to do is counteract the melancholia and its feelings of loss and guilt by creatively revisiting the site or rather sites of loss, which are no longer external but have become internalized, have been absorbed in the artist's own self-image. I am using the plural, 'sites of loss', rather than the singular because, as we saw earlier, there is another loss lurking in the deeper parts of Rabindranath's unconscious, another cut-off part of the self, which, too, finds an expression in his work: the loss of his mother.

The women's faces, then, are not only of Kadambri but also of his mother and, in having become a part of his own unconscious self-image, of Rabindranath himself. In other words, the melancholy in the female portraits is Rabindranath's own and the empathy with which he paints the women lets us look into recesses of his own psyche. It is in these female portraits more than any other creative expressions that Rabindranath sought to ease his unconscious disquiets, reintegrate the cut-off parts of the self from his early life that rose to the surface in his old age.

Such attempts at self-healing have been shown to be common in the lives of many creative geniuses in the West and indeed have been attested to by the artists themselves. The German poet Rainer

Maria Rilke wrote: 'my work is really nothing but a self treatment.'[29] Similarly, the novelist Graham Greene asserted that 'writing is a form of therapy; sometimes I wonder how all those who do not write, compose or paint can manage to escape madness, the melancholia, the panic fear which is inherent in the human situation.'

The self-healing is not always successful and artists sometimes exaggerate the benefit of their creativity. Art, even in the presence of considerable talent, cannot always stabilize a disintegrating personality. Artistic creativity, as the Canadian psychoanalyst Patrick Mahony observes, though potentially effective to various degrees in regulating symptoms or even providing narcissistically comforting insight, cannot produce a deep and permanent structural change in the psyche.[30]

On the other hand, it is true that for certain artists, not to write, paint, sculpt, make music may lead to a drastic psychic disintegration. Thus, though the American poet Sylvia Plath referred to 'poetry as therapy' and the English writer Virginia Woolf relied on her 'art to keep [her] head sane' both women committed suicide.[31]

To return to Rabindranath's female portraits—for me, in these portraits, the old painter is not only mourning the losses of his childhood and youth. He is also forgiving the boy Rabi for his ambivalent feelings of being abandoned by the mother (for a child, a parent's death is first and foremost an abandonment), and being compassionate with young Rabindranath's guilt at having betrayed the love of his life, Kadambari, as he now merges his own self-image with images of the two women. And in these fleeting moments of harmony with the dead women that he captures in his paintings, Rabindranath temporarily transcends existential loneliness and intimations of mortality even as he inexorably moves towards his own death, towards the 'eternal-feminine'. Perhaps better and certainly more evocatively than any psychological gloss, Rabindranath's poem 'First Sorrow' captures the essence of the female portraits.

> The path by the shadow of the forest is now covered with grass.
> On that deserted road, someone called me from behind.
> 'Don't you recognize me?'
>
> I turned back to look at him.
>
> 'I remember you, but do not recall your name.'
>
> He said, 'I am the sorrow who came to you when you were twenty-five.'
>
> The corner of his eyes revealed a spark of ray, just like moonlight on a lake.
>
> I stood there, surprised.
>
> 'Back then, you appeared like a dark monsoon cloud. Now, you look like a golden idol. Have you lost the tears of that day?' I asked.

He didn't say anything, just smiled. I realized everything was contained in that smile.

The clouds of the rainy day had learned to smile like bright sunny days of the summer.

I asked him, 'Have you preserved my youth of twenty-five?'

'Yes, I made it my necklace. Not even a single petal of the spring's garland had fallen.'

I said, 'See, how I have shrivelled with age. But my youth is still adorning your neck, as fresh as ever.'

He slowly put that necklace around my neck and said, 'Do you remember, that day you had said, you don't need consolation, you only want sorrow?'

I shrugged a little. 'Yes, I did. But it has been so long; I had forgotten about it.'

'But the one within you hadn't forgotten. Now, you must accept me,' he said.

I held his hand and said, 'How wonderful you look!'

He smiled and said, 'That which was once sorrow, is now peace.'[32]

Oscar Wilde is mistaken when he remarks 'to reveal art and conceal the artist is art's aim'.[33] However imperfectly or blurred, art does reveal the artist, bares the themes of Rabindranath's life which had an impact on the artistic creativity of his landscapes and portraits. Their historical and cultural context as also the influences of Western modern art on these paintings is a task that lies in the province of more knowledgeable art historians.

11

Conclusion: Tagore and the Riddle of Creative Genius

At the end and in the spirit of Tagore, as an intrepid explorer of his many dualities, I would like to understand his genius through a combination of Indian and Western perspectives on the extraordinary creative person. My interest here is not in the creative potential that is marked by a gift for reinterpreting what is taken for granted, a propensity to search for and resolve contradictions, an aptitude for coining metaphors and connecting unrelated ideas in a novel way. Nor am I interested in the creative mindset which is said to be domain-specific and has such features as 'wonderment, independence, nonconformity, flexibility. . . capability for relaxation,'[1] to which I would also add playfulness. My focus here is on the extraordinary creative person, the creative genius whose exceptional contributions (sometimes even across domains) are acknowledged as revolutionary and have lastingly altered the landscape of his or her domain. Rabindranath Tagore is one of these 'immortals'.

The foundational theories of Western aesthetics, of Plato and Aristotle, which have continued to influence Western notions of the genius, have linked extraordinary creativity to an extreme mental state.[2] The madness in Plato's poet was because of the gods taking over his personality and speaking through him, while the melancholy of the genius, from Aristotle onwards (who included Plato and Socrates among the melancholics), was attributed to excess of a bodily humour, black bile.[3] Indeed, in the European Middle Ages and the early modern period, melancholy, exemplified in Albrecht's Duerer's well-known portrait as a figure for genius, became the defining attribute of the creative person.

Beginning with Freud's 1910 study of Leonardo da Vinci, the admixture of mania and depression as a defining attribute of a genius was widened by psychoanalysts. Rather than a fixed psychopathological structure in the psyche, attention now focused on the creative writer's or artist's major emotional conflicts as a source for his or her creativity. The creative person expresses and transforms these conflicts—that have their source in his or her childhood and early youth—in his or her work, poetry, music or art while at the same time the creativity and the creative product buffer him or her from the trauma inherent in the emotional conflict. The latter function of creativity, providing a haven from the storms of emotional life, is not limited to artists but may well extend to all highly creative individuals. As Albert Einstein observes, 'This is what the painter does, and the poet, the speculative philosopher, the natural scientist, each in his own way. Into this [simplified and lucid] image of the world and its formation, he places the center of gravity of his emotional life, in order to attain the peace and serenity that he cannot find within the narrow confines of swirling personal experience.'[4]

More recent psychoanalytic contributions to the creative personality have highlighted factors other than emotional conflict: the availability, beyond childhood, of 'transitional' space (Winnicott) where play and creativity have their home; 'self-effectance' or the faith in one's own genius, which is then an autonomous source of self-esteem; the functioning of the artwork as a 'selfobject' (Kohut), enhancing the creative personality's psychic integration and sense of being alive; as also the 'mirroring' appreciation of the audience which performs the same function.[5] And though the special nature of his perception and cognition are currently receiving the greatest attention, for me, the compelling *story* of a genius remains a narration of his developmental experiences that were vital for the flowering of his creativity.

My psychobiography thus attempts to identify and reflect upon the formative events of Tagore's emotional life: the traumatic exile from the maternal universe, the sanctuary the child found in the gift of a highly creative imagination that went unnoticed for a time, the humiliation of school years and the shakiness in his budding sense of identity, the feeling of 'self-effectance' and the recognition received from significant people in exercising his gift of poetry in later childhood, the tolerance of the son's poetic 'waywardness' by the father, the finding of deep intimacy in adolescence that not only garbed his soul in erotic grace but lent cohesion to his self and reaffirmed his identity both as a man and a poet, the loss of this intimacy with the suicide of the 'soulmate' and the subsequent effect of mourning in his life and creative work. I am aware that although this line of enquiry may produce a satisfactory and, indeed, even an enlightening account of the creative person's inner life, it is not sufficient to account for his genius. Psychobiography can bring the subject to life, give human face to a genius, but its contribution to the explanation of his or her extraordinary creativity is limited.

Contemporary contributions to the riddle of artistic creativity seek to complement the role of emotions (when they do not replace it altogether), which biography can bring out vividly, with the special nature of the artist's cognitive and perceptual processes that have their source in the brain; the shift is from the psyche of the creative personality to its soma. In other words, creativity is viewed by many as fundamentally biological. Indeed, together with the mystery of consciousness, the riddle of creativity is currently the holy grail of biology.

For instance, synesthesia, the blending of senses, is said to be seven to eight times more in artists than in the rest of the population. What synesthesia does is increase skill in forming metaphors, the linking of seemingly unrelated concepts in the brain. The neuroscientist V.S. Ramachandran suggests that there may be a gene which, if expressed in one part of the brain, fusiform gyrus, results in lower synesthesia. If expressed in another part, in the angular gyrus, it results in higher synesthesia. If expressed all over the brain, you get the potential artist.[6] There is also evidence that artists can shift between brain hemispheres more fluidly than non-artists and that creativity may be enhanced when inter-hemispheric flexibility is maximized. And though there are influential voices, such as those of the philosopher McGinn, who argue that the explanation of high level thought and consciousness is as far beyond the cognitive capacities of *Homo sapiens* as theoretical physics is beyond the capacities of squirrels and chimpanzees, there is a widespread belief that neurosciences hold the key to the understanding of extraordinary creativity.[7] Creativity is not mysterious and as the Nobel Laureate Pete Medawar observes, the idea that 'creativity is beyond analysis is a romantic illusion we must now outgrow'.[8] At the most, contemporary research on creativity concedes that unlocking its secrets is not solely a scientific endeavour but will also require insights from poets, writers, philosophers, psychologists and artists.[9]

Indian foundational texts on high level artistic creativity, on the other hand, take a very different tack from those of the Western tradition. From the classical text on the performing arts, Bharata's *Natya Shastra* (*ca.* 200 BC), through its authoritative interpretation in the commentary by Abhinavagupta (975–1025 AD) who also included literature and fine arts in his theory of aesthetics, to the modern works of the renowned art historian Ananda Coomaraswamy (1877–1947), there has been a unitary view of the creative artist. He is not a flawed being, prone to madness or melancholia. Not for the Indian artist the sensual excesses that Europeans have almost come to expect of their creative artists. As the ancient texts, the Shilpa Shastras, describe the Indian artist: 'the painter must be a good man, no sluggard, nor given to anger; holy, learned, self-controlled, devout and charitable' and especially not an adulterer.[10] The striving for individuality in the artist and receiving the nutrients for self-esteem from 'effectance' and appreciation from the audience, were suspicious. To be truly creative, it was necessary for the individual personality traits and complexes to be transcended. They were believed to be transitory and accidental, veiling the fount of creativity—*pratibha* or creative imagination—which is so strong in the artist that it responds to the slightest stimuli, normally ignored by others. (In contrast, the basis of scientific creativity is *prajna*—wisdom, discrimination, awareness—which is more a learnt than an innate capacity).

The Indian view diverges, even more substantially, from contemporary Western findings on creativity—not only on the role played by unconscious processes but on the nature of the unconscious itself. We now know that perhaps as much as 95 per cent of our mental life is unconscious, hidden from our consciousness which has little or no insight into the motivations that underlie our wishes and actions. Unconscious processes steer our conscious lives, including the creation and appreciation of poetry and art. The major function of our conscious awareness, besides the gathering of information where it is superior to the unconscious, may indeed be telling stories to ourselves about what we think, believe or do, thus giving them a veneer of coherence and intelligibility. Modern psychological research has also widened the view of unconscious activity, which is much richer and more varied than what was postulated by Freud. Of the different types of unconscious processes, one of the more relevant for the understanding of creativity is the cognitive unconscious—unconscious information processing which involves cognition that has a ready access to both consciousness, and to what Freud called the dynamic unconscious: emotional conflicts, repressed wishes, thoughts and actions.

The classical Indian view on artistic creativity, shared and elaborated on by Tagore, is silent on the kind of unconscious processes that are at the centre of modern psychological and neuroscience research. In the Indian view, creative imagination has access to a transcendent, spiritual unconscious that lies in a deeper layer of the mind than the strata in which the cognitive, dynamic and other unconscious processes are located. At this deeper level, the spiritual unconscious is said to connect with the hidden order of the universe or, in another formulation, is united with the consciousness animating all existence. Analogous to the pleasure principle governing the Freudian dynamic unconscious, the spiritual unconscious can be said to be governed by the 'unity principle'.

Tagore attributes his creativity to this spiritual unconscious, which he calls the 'One within me' and whose creations, such as pictures, poems, music, are a pastime through which it finds joy only because they reveal the perfect forms of an inherent unity. 'This One not only seeks unity in knowledge for its understanding and creates images of unity for its delight, it also seeks union in love for its fulfillment.'[11] Art, music or poetry that come into being in response to the fulfilment of the artist's emotional needs is merely constructive whereas the joy of unity within him seeking expression, is creative; artistic creativity is the translation of this truth into our own symbols.

For Tagore, creative imagination, which 'makes songs not only with words and tunes, lines and colours, but with stones and metals, with ideas and men', is the common truth both in a human being and in the heart of existence. Since the spiritual unconscious lies beyond conscious awareness, great artists, writers and music makers have often felt that their inspiration comes from *outside* themselves, that it is not self-centred. Considered almost a truism in India, this has also been the position of many artists and writers in the

West in the pre-modern era though their modern counterparts are reluctant to openly embrace such a 'spiritual' outlook. In his Nobel Prize acceptance speech, Saul Bellow observes, 'The sense of our real powers, powers we seem to derive from the universe itself, also comes and goes. . .We are reluctant to talk about this because there is nothing we can prove, because our language is inadequate, and because few people are willing to risk talking about it. They would have to say that there is a spirit, and that is taboo.'[12] Pre-modern geniuses, certainly in India, had no such inhibitions. Mirza Ghalib, the great nineteenth century Urdu poet, could write: *Aate hain ghaibse ye / mazamiin khyal mein / Ghalib sareer e khama / navaye sarosh hai* (My thoughts come to me / From somewhere Beyond / When Ghalib is attuned / To the music of the stars.)

Do emotions, especially those evoked by our conscious and unconscious memories, play no role in the creative works of a genius? Here Tagore offers a synthesis of sorts between Indian and Western psychological approaches. The consciousness of unity in ourselves, he says, 'becomes prominently distinct when coloured by joy or sorrow, or some other emotion. . .In the creation of art, therefore, the energy of an emotional idea is necessary; as its unity is not like that of a crystal, passive and inert, but actively expressive.'[13] Without the emotional idea, *bhava*, a poem with all its perfection and proportion, rhyme and cadence, would only be a construction, would not find a synchronous response in the metre of our heartbeats.[14] Creative expressions, then, attain their perfect form through the modulation of emotions.

However, it is undeniable that for Tagore art is more than an expression of emotion, that 'A lyric is indefinably more than the sentiment expressed in it, as a rose is more than its substance.'[15] What makes the ingredients of poetry—perceptions, feelings, language—into a poem is the transformative power of the hidden creative imagination.

Ideas take shape by some hidden, subtle skill at work within the poet. This creative power is the origin of poetry. Perceptions, feelings, or language, are only raw material. One may be gifted with feeling, a second with language, a third with both; but he who has well a creative genius, alone is a poet.[16]

It is not only in poetry but also in his life that Tagore sees the work of this creative power, the Jibandebata—literally, life-god. The Jibandebata, Entheos, not only weaves fragmentary emotional processes into a continuous significance in art but in life knits up 'all the damage I undergo, piecing it together, shoring it up'.[17]

'An immense memory of a long sequence of existence continuing through this world has gathered round him, and lies in me, in my unconscious,' he writes. 'That is why I feel a kinship of such long standing with the world's flora and fauna. That is why the huge mysterious world does not seem alien and terrible.'[18] The Jibandebata not only repairs the damage in the life of a genius but opens up its limits imposed by instincts and narcissism 'and through deep pain and severance of ties, he is fusing it with what is great and cosmic'.[19] Extraordinary artistic creativity is thus neither a compensation for nor a sublimation of deep pain that reaches back into childhood. The pain only serves to open up a channel in the artist for the flow of the creative power from the spiritual unconscious that both creates and cures.

My own position is sympathetic to that of Tagore though I would emphasize a greater balance between the biological-life historical and the transcendent-spiritual unconscious in the psyche of the artistic genius than he does; in privileging the latter he may have succumbed to the temptation of underplaying the former. If I may use the Buddhist metaphor of the lotus as the symbol of creativity, a flower opening to light and sun, symbolizing the transcendent, then we also need to remember that the lotus grows in mud, the symbol of the biological-life historical unconscious. The flowering of the lotus needs the mud as much as it needs light and sun, the swirling of drives and emotions in the unconscious as much as the sat-chit-ananda. The mud is not dirt, but as a mix of the elements of earth and water, it is also the soil of creativity from which the lotus soars above the ground into sunlight. One does not have to fully subscribe to either the sun or mud views on origins of extraordinary creativity but pay greater attention to the stem, where both the transcendent-spiritual and the biological-emotional flow into each other.

Notes

1   In creativity research, it has been variously called 'transformational', to distinguish it from 'exploratory' or 'combinatory' creativity (Boden) or Big-C creativity as separate from little-c creativity (Csikszentmihalyi); see M.A. Boden, *Creativity and Art: Three Roads to Surprise*, Oxford: Oxford University Press, 2010, and M. Csikszentmihalyi, *Creativity: Flow and the Psychology of Discovery and Invention*, New York: Harper Collins, 1996.

1. INTRODUCTION: WRITING THE BIOGRAPHY OF INNER LIFE

1   R. Tagore, *My Reminiscences*, tr. S.N. Tagore, New York: The Macmillan Company, 1917, 1–3. The Bengali original, *Jibansmriti*, was published in 1911 though there is evidence that Tagore had begun writing portions of it some years earlier; cf. Footnote 5, Chapter Two. The second autobiographical sketch is *Boyhood Days*, tr. R. Chakravarty, Delhi: Puffin, 2007. The Bengali original, *Chhelebela*, was published sometime in August–September 1940. Tagore began writing this account in April of that year, a year before his death at the age of eighty; see the translator's note, 91. There are scattered memories also in *Of Myself* (Atamaparichay), tr. D. Joardar and J. Winter, Shantiniketan: Visva-Bharati, 2006, a series of essays on his poetic and philosophical development, written between the ages of fifty and seventy and published posthumously in 1943.

Tagore's childhood memories were never as vivid and compelling as in the couple of years before his death, captured not only in *Boyhood Days* but also in many poems published in 1939 in the volume *Akashradip* (The Lamp in the Sky).

2   Of biographies of literary figures, the ones that come immediately to my mind are Richard Ellman's masterly 1959 biography of James Joyce and, of a more recent vintage, David Lodge's 2011 biography of H.G. Wells.

3   Indeed, the root word of speculation, speculum, also means the mirror. Psychobiographical speculation can then be said to have the quality of seeing in a mirror darkly, as in the classic quotation from St. Paul in the first letter to the Corinthians: *'videmus nunc per speculum in aenigmate'*—now we see in a mirror darkly. Freud's musing, 'One must reflect that what is probable is not necessarily the truth and that the truth is not always probable' is very apt here; cf. S. Freud (1939), 'Moses and Monotheism', in J. Strachey, ed., *The Standard Edition of the Complete Psychological Works of Sigmund Freud*, vol. 23, London: Hogarth Press, 1953–74, 17.

4   For an illustration of the wide variety of approaches see J.A. Winer and J.W. Anderson, eds., 'Psychoanalysis and History', *Annual of Psychoanalysis*, XXXI, Hillsdale, NJ: Analytic Press, 2003; For a methodological overview see, J.E. Gedo, 'The Methodology of Psychoanalytic Biography,' *J. Am. Psychoanal. Assn.*, 20, 1972, 638–49; See also M. Bergman, 'Limitations of Method in Psychoanalytic Biography: A Historical Inquiry', *J. Am. Psychoanal Assn.*, 21, 1973, 833–50 ; E.H. Erikson, 'On the Nature of 'Psycho-Historical Evidence', in *Life History and the Historical Moment*, New York: Norton, 1975, 113–68.

5   S. Freud (1936), 'Letter to Arnold Zweig, May 31', in E. Freud, ed., *The Letters of Sigmund Freud*, New York: Harcourt Brace Jovanovich, 1970, 136.

6   S. Freud (1910), 'Leonardo da Vinci and a Memory of his Childhood', *Standard Edition*, vol. 11, London: Hogarth Press, 130.

7   See my *The Book of Memory*, Delhi: Penguin, 2011.

8   L. Strachey, 'Macaulay', in *Portraits in Miniature: and Other Essays*, London: Chatto and Windus, 1931, 170. T.S. Eliot has something similar in mind when he remarks, 'Sometimes a critic may choose an author to criticize, as far as possible the antithesis of himself, a personality which has actualized all that has been suppressed in himself; we can sometimes arrive at a very satisfactory intimacy with our anti masks'; see his *The Uses of Poetry and the Uses of Criticism*, Cambridge, Mass.: Harvard University Press, 104.

9   Indeed, the failure of Freud's psychological study of Woodrow Wilson is
     primarily due to his dislike of the American president. See S. Freud and W.
     C. Bullitt, *Thomas Woodrow Wilson: Twenty-Eighth President of the United States.
     A Psychological Study*, Boston: Houghton Mifflin, 1967.
10   *Boyhood Days*, 87.

2. THE PARADISE

1   R. Tagore, *Stray Birds*, tr. by author, No. 182, New York, Macmillan, 1916.
2   *Reminiscences*, 257–59.
3   William Wordsworth, *The Prelude*, III, 645–8, cited in D. Aberbach, 'Screen
     Memories of Writers', *International Review of Psychoanalysis*, 10, 1983, 59.
4   Cited in Aberbach, 60.
5   From the two authoritative biographies in Bengali, Prashanta K. Paul's
     Rabijibani (5 vols) and Prabhat Kumar Mukhopadhaya's *Rabindra-Jibani o
     Rabindra-Sahitya* (4 vols), the best available information is that some of the
     Jibansmriti writings were already published in the Bengali literary journal
     Probashi which he was reading out in 1910. Some other parts that reflect his
     later collection in *Jibansmriti* were published in *Bangabhasha*, another literary
     journal, around 1906.
6   Chitra Deb, *Women of the Tagore Household*, tr. S. Chowdhry and S. Roy, Delhi:
     Penguin, 16–19.
7   *Ibid.*, 16.
8   *Ibid.*, 3.
9   *Boyhood Days*, 21.
10   *Ibid.*, 23.
11   *Ibid.*, 49.
12   F.W. Nietzsche, *Beyond Good and Evil*, NP: New Vision, 2007, 12.
13   See also Aberbach, 47–62; K. Oatley & A. Kerr, 'Memories Prompted by
     Emotions—Emotions attached to Memories', *Journal of American Academy
     of Psychoanalysis and Dynamic Psychiatry*, 27(4), 1999, 657–69; T.J. Scheff,
     Catharsis in Healing, Ritual and Drama, Berkeley, CA: University of California
     Press,1979.
14   *Reminiscences*, 212.
15   Most of the poems were written in 1903 and appeared in the volume *Shishu*

(The Infant). They were translated into English by the author and published
as *The Crescent Moon*, London: Macmillan, 1924.

16 See my *The Inner World: A Psychoanalytic Study of Childhood and Society*, Delhi
and New York: Oxford University Press, 1978, 78–9.

17 See the editor's note on 'Dear Mother' in R. Tagore, *Selected Poems*, ed. S.
Choudhuri, New Delhi: Oxford University Press, 2004, 402.

18 *Reminiscences*, 220.

19 *Ibid.*, 72.

20 These are Karna's words to his long lost mother Kunti on hearing her
voice in Tagore's play, *Karna and Kunti*, in *The Fugitive*, New York: Macmillan,
1921, 178.

21 'Baby's World,' in *Crescent Moon*, 17.

22 'When and Why', *Crescent Moon*, 18–19.

23 'The Beginning', *Crescent Moon*, 15–16.

24 'Clouds and Waves', *Crescent Moon*, 28.

25 'The Champa Flower', *Crescent Moon*, 29–30.

26 'The Baby's Way', *Crescent Moon*, 7–8.

27 'Sympathy', *Crescent Moon*, 49.

28 'The Sailor', *Crescent Moon*, 41.

29 'The Further Bank', *Crescent Moon*, 42–44.

30 'The Hero', *Crescent Moon*, 62–65.

31 *Women of the Tagore Household*, 18.

32 'The Wicked Postman', *Crescent Moon*, 60–1. See also the poem 'Authorship'
(pp.58–9) where the child tries to make the mother doubt the value of his
father writing books.

33 'The Little Big Man', *Crescent Moon*, 54.

34 'The End', *Crescent Moon*, 66.

35 *Reminiscences*, 7–8.

36 *Reminiscences*, 75. There is a glorification of childhood innocence in this
passage, an unwillingness to reflect on his own erotic sensuality of early
childhood that, instead, seeps through in the poems of mother and child in
The Crescent Moon. But, then, as he writes at the end of the very next passage,
'The fact is that what goes on in the inner recesses of consciousness is not
always known to the surface dweller.'

3. THE EXILE

1   *Reminiscences*, 8, 12–13.

2   *Ibid.*, 25.

3   *Ibid.*, 26.

4   *Boyhood Days*, 33–35.

5   *Reminiscences*, 10.

6   *Boyhood Days*, 19–21.

7   *Reminiscences*, 28.

8   *Ibid.*, 8.

9   *Ibid.*, 101–2.

10 *Boyhood Days*, 16–17

11 *Reminiscences*, 9.

12 *Boyhood Days*, 113.

13 *Ibid.*, 27.

14 *Ibid.*, 30.

15 *Reminiscences*, 102.

16 *Ibid.*, 103–4

17 *Ibid.*, 104.

18 R. Tagore, 'The Home Coming', in *Selected Stories,* 2009, 24.

19 *Ibid.*, 26.

20 R. Tagore,' The Postmaster', in *The Postmaster: Selected Stories*, tr. W. Radice, Delhi: Penguin, 1991, 46–47.

21 *Reminiscences*, 238.

22 *Boyhood Days*, 13–14.

23 R.J. Stoller, *Perversion*, New York: Pantheon, 1975, 55.

24 See my 'The Resurgence of Imagination', in *Harvard Divinity School Bulletin,* 37(1), 2009, ?

25 D.W. Winnicott, 'The Capacity to be Alone', *Int. J. Psychoanal.*, 39, 1958, 416–20.

26 S. Kierkegaard, *The Concept of Dread*, tr. W. Lowrie, Princeton: Princeton University Press, 1944, 107.

27 'My Song', *Crescent Moon*, 78.

28 F. Fromm-Reichmann, 'Loneliness', *Contemporary Psychoanalysis*, 26, 1990, 305–29.

29 Letter to C.F. Andrews, 21 December 1920, *Tagore Archives*, Rabindra Bhavan, Shantiniketan.

30 Letter to C.F. Andrews, March 1921.

31 Letter to Rani Mahanalobis, 28 October 1929. Translated by Jhuma Basak.

32 Letter to Andrews, 11 October 1913.

33 Letter to Indira Devi, 24 September 1894. Tr. J. Basak.

34 Letter to Rani Mahalanobis, September 1929. Tr. J. Basak.

35 Letter to Rani Mahalanobis, July 1929. Tr. J. Basak

36 Letter to Rani Mahalanobis, 11 July 1935. Tr. J. Basak.

4. The Terrace and the Inner Garden

1 *Boyhood Days*, 52.

2 *Reminiscences*, 14–15.

3 *Boyhood Days*, 50.

4 *Ibid.*, 53–54.

5 *Ibid.*, 54.

6 See R. F. Hobson, 'Loneliness', *J. Anal. Psychol.*, 19, 1974, 71–89.; T. Parkinson, 'Loneliness of the Poet', in J. Hartog, J.R. Audy and Y.A. Cohen eds., *The Anatomy of Loneliness*, New York: Int. University Press, 1980, 467–85.

7 R. Tagore, 'Fruit-Gathering', in *The Fugitive*, London: Macmillan, 1918, 81.

8 The title of Rabindranath's well-known novel, *The Home and the World*.

9 C.G. Jung, 'Psychology and Literature', in *Modern Man in Search of a Soul*, tr. W.S. Dell and C.F. Baynes, San Diego: Harcourt Brace Jovanovich, 1933, 168.

10 Letter to C.F. Andrews, 7 September 1915.

11 *Reminiscences*, 271–2.

12 Letter to Indira Devi, February 1893.

13 F. Nietzsche, *Daybreak*, tr. R.J. Hollingdale, Cambridge: Cambridge University Press, 1982, 201.

14 *Reminiscences*, 17–18.

15 R. Tagore, 'The Poet's Religion', in *Creative Unity*, London: Macmillan, 1922, 9.

16 *Reminiscences*, 163. Here Rabindranath's view is similar to that of Mark Twain who believed that human minds send out signals and an original idea might

not be original but is plucked out of air by a sensitive mind; see J.J. Kripal, 'Introduction: Thinking Anew about Psychical experiences', in S. Kakar and J.J. Kripal, eds, *Seriously Strange*, Delhi: Penguin-Viking, 2012, xviii–xix.

17 S.K. Das, *The English Writings of Tagore, Vol. I: Poems*, Delhi: Sahitya Akademi, 2004, 353.

18 I owe this interpretation to Patrick Mahony's comment on the poem.

19 E.H. Erikson, *Life History and the Historical Moment*, New York: Norton, 1975, 160.

20 *Reminiscences*, 259–60.

21 Letter to C.F. Andrews, 28 March 1921.

22 Hobson, 74.

23 *Reminiscences*, 226.

5. A PAINFUL WELCOME TO THE WORLD

1 *Reminiscences*, 233.

2 *Boyhood Days*, 44–5.

3 *Ibid.*, 45.

4 *Ibid.*, 46.

5 *Reminiscences*, 41.

6 *Boyhood Days*, 47.

7 *Ibid.*

8 *Reminiscences*, 41–2.

9 *Ibid.*, 59–60.

10 *Reminiscences*, 60–1.

11 S. Kakar and K. Kakar, *The Indians: Portrait of a People*, New Delhi: Viking, 2007, 98–201.

12 *Reminiscences*, 33.

13 *Ibid.*, 60.

14 *Of Myself*, 51.

15 *Reminiscences.*, 63.

16 *Ibid.*, 66.

17 *Ibid.*, 33

18 *Ibid.*, 225.

19 *Ibid.*, 36.

20 *Ibid.*, 53.

21 Letter to Indira Devi, March 1893. Tr. J. Basak.

22 *Reminiscences*, 85.

23 *Ibid.*

24 Letter to Andrews, 30 November 1920.

25 Letter to Andrews, 23 February 1921.

26 Letter to Andrews, 9 July 1917.

27 Letter to Andrews, undated, probably March 1921.

28 Letter to Andrews, undated, probably April 1921.

29 Letter to Andrews, 26 February 1921.

30 Letter to Andrews, 9 July 1921.

31 Letter to Andrews, undated.

6. THE WAY OF THE FATHER

1   D. Tagore, *The Autobiography of Maharshi Devendranath Tagore*, tr. S.N. Tagore
    and Indira Devi, London: Macmillan, 1916, 35.

2   *Ibid.*, 38.

3   *Ibid.*, 40.

4   *Ibid.*, 45.

5   *Ibid.*, 102.

6   *Ibid.*, 75.

7   *Ibid.*

8   *Ibid.*, 145.

9   *Ibid.*, 262.

10 *Reminiscences*, 90.

11 *Ibid.*, 81.

12 *Ibid.*, 87.

13 *Ibid.*, 95.

14 This outburst came in a discussion with Gandhi who had defended idol
    worship by the masses as 'the only tangible symbol of God our half-starved
    brother has ever had. How can we deny him the only link between himself
    and God?'; cited in P.K. Mukopadhyay, *Rabindra Jibani*, 3rd edn., Calcutta,
    Visva-Bharati, 1991, 236.

15 R. Tagore, *Letters from a Sojourner in Europe*, tr. M. Chakravarty, Shantiniketan: Visva-Bharati, 2008, 125.

16 *Ibid.*

17 *Reminiscences*, 101.

7. KADAMBARI AND THE SMELL OF BUTTERED TOAST

1 *Boyhood Days*, 60. Debendranath had left Jorasanko to live away from the family in their Park Street residence in south Calcutta.

2 *Ibid.*, 57.

3 *Ibid.*, 58.

4 *Ibid.*, 57.

5 Deb, 79.

6 Dutta and Robinson, Rabindranath Tagore: The Myriad-minded Man, 80.

7 J. Bhattacharya, *Kobimanushi*, vol. 2, Calcutta: Bharbi, 2000, 158. Tr. J. Basak.

8 *Boyhood Days.*, 62–63.

9 *Ibid.*, 66–67.

10 *Ibid.*, 58.

11 Deb, 84. Rabindranath writes that Kadambari had impressed upon him 'that, generally speaking my cranium and features, compared with those of many another, were barely of average standard'; cf. *Reminiscences*,15. Biharilal Chakravarty was a lyrical poet. Kadambari's admiration for his highly romantic songs led her to invite him often to their house and to embroider a cushion-seat for him with her own hands. Needless to add, that for Rabi, 'The height of my ambition at the time was to become a poet like Bihari Babu'; cf. *Reminiscences*,125.

12 Nirmal Kumari Mahalanobis, *Baishey Sravan*, Calcutta: Mitra & Ghosh, 2011, Tr. J. Basak.

13 *Reminiscences*, 133.

14 In a series of biographical studies, Howard Gardner observes that both are required by a creator during a time of artistic or intellectual breakthrough; cf. H. Gardner, *Creating Minds*, New York: Basic Books, 1993.

15 *Reminiscences*,148.

16 Letter to Andrews, 28 March 1921.

17 Letter to Indira Devi, 5 July 1894
18 *Boyhood Days*, 77.
19 *Reminiscences*, 178.
20 *Ibid.*
21 *Ibid.*, 182.
22 *Ibid.*, 181.
23 Tagore, *Creative Unity*, 51.
24 Letter to Rani Mahalanobis, 14 March 1929. Emphasis added. Tr. J. Basak.

8. THE PASSAGE TO ENGLAND

1   *Boyhood Days*, 82–83.
2   *Ibid.*, 85. That Ana was deeply affected by Rabi is also evidenced by the fact that even after her marriage to a Scotsman and living in Edinburgh, she continued to use Nalini as her literary nom de plume. One of her nephews was named Rabindranath, after the poet.
3   *Ibid.*, 90. Rabi is another name for the sun that shines on East and West alike.
4   *Reminiscences*, 152.
5   Although Prabhat Mukhhopadhaya feels that all the letters were written to Kadambari, I am inclined to agree with Jagdish Bhattacharya that apart from letters 4, 6, 10 and 12 (and on internal evidence, I would also add letter 7 that has a man as its addressee), the others were addressed to Kadambari; see R. Tagore, *Letters from a Sojourner in Europe*, 13.
6   *Letters from a Sojourner in Europe*, 48.
7   *Ibid.*, 157.
8   *Ibid.*, 171.
9   *Ibid.*, 172.
10 *Ibid.*, 25–26
11 *Ibid.*, 33.
12 *Ibid.*, 25–26.
13 *Ibid.*, 38.
14 *Ibid.*, 41.
15 *Ibid.*, 43.
16 *Ibid.*, 45.
17 *Ibid.*

18 *Ibid.*

19 Dutta and Robinson, 75. In his poem *Two Days*, which he wrote on his
    return to Calcutta, he writes of his parting from the girls, especially Lucy
    who taught him to sing English songs and who he tutored in Bengali. The
    last three verses, in Krishna Kriplani's translation, read:

> This face, made as if a million flowers had gone into
> Its making and this hair loose and disheveled will
> Haunt my sleep night after night and these eyes wistful
> With longing will look into mine and a voice broken
> With tears will whisper, 'Must you leave, must you?'

> The two-day sojourn is over,
> The leafless tree had no time to blossom, the snow
> Had no time to melt. And yet this two-day interlude
> Will for ever hold me in its arms, its feel will
> Never fade from my life.

> And O the regret and shame of it!
> I came for two days to this land—only to break
> A gentle heart!

See *Letters from a Sojourner in Europe*, 17–18.

20 *Ibid.*, 130–31.
21 *Ibid.*, 118–19.
22 *Ibid.*, 139–40.
23 Letter to Andrews, 16 October 1913.
24 Letter to Andrews, July 1918.
25 Letter to Andrews on board *S.S. Rhyndam*, undated, probably March 1921.
26 Tagore, *Creative Unity*, 195.
27 *Ibid.*
28 *Ibid.*, 84
29 M.K. Gandhi, *The Collected Works of Mahatma Gandhi*, New Delhi:
    Government of India Publications Division, 1999, vol. 56, 286.
30 *Ibid.*, vol. 36, 5.
31 Tagore, *Creative Unity*, 49.

32 Letter to Andrews, undated, probably first week of April 1921.

33 *Creative Unity*, 120.

34 *Ibid.*, 122.

35 *Ibid.*, 76.

36 *Ibid.*

37 *Ibid.*, 86.

38 *Ibid.*, 75.

39 *Ibid.*, 86–87.

40 *Ibid.*, 87.

41 Environmental psychology, as it exists today, focuses on the effect of (a restricted view of) environment primarily on behaviour. See D. Stokols and I. Altman, eds, *Handbook of Psychology*, New York: Wiley, 1987; M. Bonnes and G. Secchiaroli, *Environmental Psychology: A Psycho-social Introduction*, London: Sage, 1995.

42 Tagore, *Creative Unity*, 51.

43 H. Arendt, 'Reflections on Violence,' *New York Review of Books*, 12, 1969, 20.

44 Letter to Andrews, 9 July 1921.

45 Letter to Andrews, 23 September 1925.

46 Letter to Andrews, 7 July 1915.

47 Letter to Andrews, 9 September 1920.

9. THE FALLING OF THE SHADOW

1 *Reminiscences*, 198.

2 *Ibid.*, 208–9.

3 Letter to Promatha Chowdhry, 29 May, 1890, *Chithipatra*, vol. 5. 132–33.

4 R. Tagore, *Selected Poems*, 47–49.

5 Cited in R. Datta and C. Seely, *Celebrating Tagore: A Collection of Essays*, 2009, 227.

6 *Reminiscences*, 200–1.

7 *Ibid.*, 212.

8 *Rabindra-Jibani*. Mukhopadhaya writes: 'That star of the poet is the guiding star. That star is Kadambari Devi. Before the final offering of her life, Kadambari Devi had attempted suicide once before. The birth of the poem, 'Death of a Star' is assumed to be from that incident.'

9   R. Tagore, *Selected Poems*, 43–44. In original Bengali, the gender of the star
     is unspecified.

10   *Reminiscences*, 215.

11   *Ibid.*, 216.

12   R. Tagore, *Selected Poems* 45–46.

13   *Ibid.*, 379.

14   S. K. Das, ed., *The English Writings of Rabindranath Tagore*, New Delhi, vol.
     3, 1996, 121. Emphasis added.

15   Dutta and Robinson, 86.

16   Cited in Dutta and Robinson, 104–5.

17   *Reminiscences*, 241.

18   Deb, 95.

19   R. Tagore, *Three Novellas*, tr. S. Ray, New Delhi: Oxford University Press,
     2010, 5.

20   *Ibid.*, 57.

21   Tagore writing in *Pushpanjali*, cited in Deb, 91.

22   *Reminiscences*, 260–61.

23   *Ibid.*, 262.

24   *Ibid.*

25   Letter to Rathindranath Tagore, 25 September 1914, *Chithipatra*, vol. 2, 31–34.
     Emphases are Rabindranath's own. Tr. J. Basak.

26   R. Tagore, *The Home and the World*, tr. S. Tagore, New Delhi: Penguin, 1999,
     40–41.

27   Letter to Andrews, 21 May 1914.

28   Letter to Andrews, 25 May 1914.

29   Letter to Andrews, 31 January 1915.

30   Letter to Andrews, 1 February 1915.

31   Tagore, *Stray Birds*, no. 321.

32   The original hypothesis of Freud in his 1916 paper 'Those Wrecked by
     Success', *Standard Edition.*, 14, 316–31, has been elaborated by other
     psychoanalytic writers; see S.T. Levy, B.J. Seelig and L.B. Inderbitzin, 'On
     those Wrecked by Success: a Clinical Inquiry,' *Psychoanal Q.*, 64(4), 1995,
     639–57. M. Friedman, 'Towards a Reconceptualization of Guilt,' *Cont.
     Psychoanal.* 21, 1985, 501–47. See also A.H. Modell, 'The Origins of Certain
     Forms of pre-Oedipal Guilt and the Implications for a Psychoanalytic Theory

of Affects.' *Int. J. Psychoanal.*, 52, 1971, 337–46.

33 R. Tagore, 'Tumi ki keboli chobi?' (Are you a mere picture?), *Balaka* (Wild Geese), 1914.

34 *The Home and the World*, 188–89.

35 Letter to Andrews, 17 May 1914.

36 Letter to Andrews, 29 January 1915.

37 Letter to Andrews, 24 May 1914.

38 Letter to Andrews, 3 February 1915.

39 W. Niederland, 'Psychoanalytic Approaches to Artistic Creativity,' *Psychoanal. Q.*, 45, 1976, 193–95.

10. ART AND PSYCHE: THE PAINTINGS

1   J. Coltrera, ' Review of "The Artist and the Emotional World" by John Gedo', *J. Amer. Psychoanal. Assn.*, 1998, 46, 1303.

2   A. Dutta, 'Tagore: Its for My Pictures to Express and Not to Explain,' *The Hindu*, 17 July 2010.

3   K. Roy, 'Rabindranath Tagore's Emergence as an Artist,' in *Rabindranath Thakur*, New Delhi: National Gallery of Modern Art, 1988, 53.

4   The term ,spiritual' as distinct from 'religious' is first encountered in the nineteenth century in the writings of Ralph Waldo Emerson.

5   *Glimpses of Bengal*, 30.

6   Dutta and Robinson, 355

7   *Of Myself*, 68.

8   A. Coomaraswamy, *The Transformation of Nature into Art*, Delhi: Munshiram Manoharlal, 2010, 7–8.

9   Cited in Roy, 51.

10 Cited in Coomaraswamy, *Transformation of Nature into Art*, 8.

11 Gilbert Rose, *Necessary Illusion: Art as Witness*, Madison, CT: IUP, 1996, 32.

12 L.S. Vygotsky, *The Psychology of Art*, Cambridge, MA.: MIT Press, 1971, 37.

13 Cited in Indrani Sengupta, 'Reflections on Paintings of Rabindranath Tagore', *http://easternpanorama.in/index.php?option=com_content&view=article&id= 1136:reflection-on-paintings-of-rabindranath-tagore&catid=61:september*

14 *Ibid.*

15 *Ibid.*

16 Roy, 49.

17 Cited in Roy, 50.

18 *Ibid.*, 52.

19 Letter to Rani Mahalanobis, 7 November 1928. Tr. J. Basak.

20 Albert Rothenberg has emphasized the importance of 'Janusian thought', the simultaneous conception of antithetical ideas or images in the work of highly creative persons. See A. Rothenburg, *The Emerging Goddess: The Creative Process in Art, Science, and Other Fields*, Chicago: University of Chicago Press,1979. In support of the notion, he observes that for Coleridge the 'pleasure arising from art consisted of the identity of two opposite elements…' (144). For Robert Graves, poetry arose from 'the unforeseen fusion in [the poet's]… mind of apparently contradictory ideas' (193).

21 The quotes are from V. Shahly, 'Pregnant with Joy and Sorrow: Creativity, Androgyny, and Manic-Depression', *Annual of Psychoanalysis*, 1988, 16, 289–318.

22 E.H. Erikson, Unpublished comments on Tagore in a seminar on *The Human Life Cycle*, Ahmedabad, 1964.

23 *Ibid.*

24 Roy, .

25 *Of Myself*, 49.

26 *Ibid.*, 42.

27 H. Banerjee, *Rabindranath Tagore*, New Delhi, 1971, 154

28 'Tumi ki keboli chobi?', *Balaka*.

29 Cited in Shahly, 313–14.

30 P. Mahony, personal communication, 4 July 2012.

31 Shaly, 313.

32 'First Sorrow', tr. Bhaswati Ghosh, *http://athomewriting.blogspot.de/2007/01/first-sorrow-by-rabindranath-tagore.html*

33 O. Wilde, 'Preface' to *The Picture of Dorian Gray*, New York: Pocket Books, 2005, 3.

11. Conclusion: Tagore and the Riddle of Creative Genius

1   E. Kandel, *The Age of Insight: The Quest to Understand the Unconscious in Art, Mind, and Brain, from Vienna 1900 to the Present*, New York: Random House, 2012. E-book, loc 6533.

2   See G. Blamberger, 'Creativity as Experience and Process: On Myths and New Concepts of Creativity', in S. Kakar, ed., *Creativity and Imagination*, New Delhi: Penguin-Viking (forthcoming).

3   'Why is it that all those who have become eminent in philosophy or politics or poetry or the arts are clearly of an atrabilious temperament, and some of them to such an extent as to be affected by diseases caused by black bile, as is said to have happened to Heracles among the heroes?' (Aristotle, *Problemata* XXX.1 953a10–14).

4   Cited in G. Holton, *Thematic Origins of Scientific Thought*, Cambridge, Mass.: Harvard University Press, 1973, 377.

5   Beginning with Freud, the psychoanalytic literature on the creative process and the creative person is vast. Some of the more recent books, besides the works of Rose and Rothenberg already mentioned, are: G. Hagman, *The Artist's Mind: A Psychoanalytic Perspective on Creativity, Modern Art and Modern Artists*, London and New York: Routledge, 2010 ; J. Oremland, *The Origins and Psychodynamics of Creativity: A Psychoanalytic Perspective,* Madison, CT: Int. U. Press, 1997; J. Gedo, *The Artist and the Emotional world: Creativity and Personality*, New York: Columbia University Press, 1996.

6   V.S. Ramachandran and W. Hirstein, 'The Science of Art: A neurological Theory of Aesthetic Experience', *Journal of Consciousness Studies*, 6(6–7), 1999, 15–51; V.S. Ramachandran and E.M. Hubbard, 'Synaesthesia: A Window into Perception, Thought and Language', *Journal of Consciousness Studies*, 8(12), 2001, 3–34.

7   See M. Boden, 'Creativity as a Neuroscientific Mystery', Unpublished paper presented at the symposium on Creativity and Imagination, Breuninger Foundation, Wasan Island, Ontario, Canada, 17–21 July 2012.

8   Cited in H. Gardener, *Creating Minds*, 36.

9   Kandel.

10 Cited in A. Coomaraswamy, *The Dance of Shiva*, Delhi: Manohar, 2009, 26.

11 *Creative Unity*,VI. Although Tagore's views on artistic creativity will find some support in the writings of a few Western philosophers such as Gadamer, Heidegger and Maritan, I can think of only one psychoanalyst, R.D. Chessick, who will find them congenial to his own thought; see R.D. Chessick, 'What Grounds Creativity?', *J. Amer. Acad. Psychoanal.*, 33, 2005, 7–28.

12 Cited in J.A. Knight, 'The Spiritual as a Creative Force in the Person', *J. Amer. Acad. Psychoanal.*, 15, 1987, 365.

13 Tagore, *Creative Unity*, 34.

14 *Ibid.*, 24.

15 *Ibid.*

16 Letter to Indira Devi, 10 July 1893.

17 *Of Myself*, 3.

18 *Ibid.*, 4–5.

19 *Ibid.*, 4.

Acknowledgements

To Instituitions:

— Institut Morphomata, Centre for Advanced Studies in Humanities, University of Cologne, for hosting me as a Fellow for a few weeks every summer of 2011, 2012 and 2013, where much of the writing on this book was done.

— Homi Bhabha Fellowship Council, for the award of a Senior Fellowship which enabled me to meet some of the expenses for travel and research assistance in Kolkata and Shantiniketan.

To individuals:

— I owe a great deal to Dr. Jhuma Basak whose infectious enthusiasm for Tagore and deep knowledge of his oeuvre was vital for the completion of this project. Her assistance was invaluable in giving me access to the Bengali writings on Tagore and to some of his letters, which have not been translated into English.

— I also wish to thank Professor Sushanta Datta Gupta, Vice Chancellor of Visva-Bharati, a most generous host during my visits to Shantiniketan.

— In Shantiniketan, I'd also like to acknowledge the assistance, always rendered with unfailing courtesy, by:

  • Amrit Sen, Professor of English Literature, Visva-Bharati
  • Professor Tapati Mukherjee, Director, Rabindra Bhavan

- • Ashis Hajra, Chief Librarian
- • Utpal Mitra, Section in Charge Archives Manuscripts
- • Samiran Nandy and Tapas Roy of the Photo section, and
- • Prof. Soumik Nandy Majumdar of Kala Bhawan.
— R. Sivapriya and Ambar Sahil Chatterjee, my editors at Penguin, for their keen interest and helpful suggestions
— And, finally, my wife Katha, an enduring source of love and support.

Bibliography

Aberbach, D., 'Screen Memories of Writers', *International Review of Psychoanalysis*, 10, 1983, 47-62.

Arendt, H., 'Reflections on Violence', *New York Review of Books*, 12, 1969.

Banerjee, H., *Rabindranath Tagore*, Delhi: Publications Division, Ministry of Information & Broadcasting, Government of India, 1971.

Bergman, M., 'Limitations of method in psychoanalytic biography: A historical inquiry', *J. Am. Psychoanal. Assn.*, 21, 1973, 833-50.

Bhattacharya, J., *Kobimanushi*, 2 vols., Calcutta: Bharbi, 2000.

Bhattacharya, S., *Rabindranath Tagore: An Interpretation*, Delhi: Penguin, 2011.

Boden, M.A., *Creativity and Art: Three Roads to Surprise*, Oxford: Oxford University Press, 2010.

—— 'Creativity as a neuroscientific mystery', in S. Kakar, ed., *Creativity and Imagination*, Delhi: Penguin (forthcoming).

Bonnes, M., and G. Secchiaroli, *Environmental Psychology: A Psycho-social Introduction*, London: Sage, 1995.

Bullitt, W.C., *Thomas Woodrow Wilson: Twenty-Eighth President of the United States. A Psychological Study*, Boston: Houghton Mifflin, 1967.

Chessick, R.D., 'What grounds creativity?' *J. Amer. Acad. Psychoanal.*, 33, 2005, 7-28.

Coltrera, J., 'Review of "The Artist and the Emotional World" by John Gedo', *J. Amer. Psychoanal. Assn.*, 1998, 46.

Coomaraswamy, A., *The Transformation of Nature into Art*, Delhi: Munshiram Manhoarlal, 2010.

—— *The Dance of Shiva*, Delhi: Manohar , 2009.

Csikszentmihalyi, M., *Creativity: Flow and the Psychology of Discovery and Invention*. New York: Harper Collins, 1996.

Das Gupta, U., *Rabindranath Tagore: A Biography*, Delhi: Oxford, 2004.

Deb, C., *Women of the Tagore Household*, tr. S. Chowdhry and S.Roy, Delhi: Penguin, 2010.

Dutta, A., 'Tagore: Its for my pictures to express and not to explain', *The Hindu*, July 17, 2010.

Dutta, K., and A. Robinson, *Rabindranath Tagore: The Myriad-minded Man*, London: Bloomsbury, 1995.

Eliot, T.S., *The Use of Poetry and the Use of Criticism*, Cambridge, Mass: Harvard University Press, 1933.

Erikson, E.H., ,On the Nature of "Psycho-Historical" Evidence', in *Life History and the Historical Moment,* New York: Norton, 1975, 113-68.

Freud, S., (1910), 'Leonardo da Vinci and a memory of his childhood,' in J. Strachey, ed., *The Standard Edition of the Complete Psychological Works of Sigmund Freud*, London: Hogarth Press,1953-74, vol. 11.

—— (1916)'Those wrecked by success,' *Standard Edition*, vol. 14.

—— (1939), 'Moses and Monotheism', Standard Edition, vol. 23.

—— *The Letters of Sigmund Freud*, ed., E. Freud, New York: Harcourt Brace Jovanovich, 1970.

Friedman, M. M., 'Towards a reconceptualization of guilt', *Cont. Psychoanal.* 21, 1985, 501-47.

Fromm-Reichmann, F., 'Loneliness', *Contemporary Psychoanalysis*, 26, 1990, 305-29.

Gandhi, M.K., *The Collected Works of Mahatma Gandhi*, New Delhi:

Government of India Publications Division, vol.56, 1999.

Gardner, H., *Creating Minds*, New York: Basic Books, 1993.

Gedo, J.E., 'The methodology of psychoanalytic biography,' *J. Am. Psychoanal. Assn.*, 20, 1972, 638-49.

—— *The Artist and the Emotional world: Creativity and Personality*, New York: Columbia University Press, 1996

Hagman, G., *The Artist's Mind: A Psychoanalytic Perspective on Creativity, Modern art and Modern Artists*, London and New York: Routledge, 2010.

Hobson, R. F., 'Loneliness', *J. Ana. Psychol.*, 19,1974, 71-89.

Holton, G., Thematic Origins of Scientific Thought, Cambridge, Mass.: Harvard University Press, 1973.

Jung, C.G., 'Psychology and literature' in *Modern Man in Search of a Soul*, tr. W. S. Dell & C. F. Baynes, San Diego: Harcourt Brace Jovanovich, 1933.

Kakar, S., *The Inner World: A Psychoanalytic Study of Childhood and Society*, Delhi and New York: Oxford University Press, 1978.

—— *The Book of Memory*, Delhi: Penguin, 2011.

—— 'The Resurgence of Imagination', in *Harvard Divinity School Bulletin*, 37:1, 2009.

—— and J.J. Kripal, eds., *Seriously Strange*, Delhi:Penguin-Viking, 2012.

Kandel, E., *The Age of Insight: the Quest to Understand the Unconscious in Art, Mind, and Brain, from Vienna 1900 to the Present*, New York: Random House, 2012.

—— Kierkegaard, S., *The Concept of Dread*, tr. W.Lowrie, Princeton: Princeton University Press, 1944.

Knight, R.J., 'The Spiritual as a Creative Force in the Person,' *J. Amer. Acad. Psychoanal.*, 1987, 15, 365-82.

Kriplani, K., *Rabindranath Tagore: A Biography,* Calcutta: Visva-Bharati, 1980.

Levy, S.T., B.J. Seelig & L.B. Inderbitzin, 'On those wrecked by success: a clinical inquiry,' *Psychoanal Q.*, 64(4), 1995, 639-57.

Mahalanobis, N. K., *Baishey Sravan*, Calcutta: Mitra & Ghosh, 2011.

Modell, A.H., 'The origins of certain forms of pre-Oedipal guilt and the implications for a psychoanalytic theory of affects.' *Int. J. Psychoanal.*, 52, 1971, 337-46.

Mukhopadhyay, P. K., *Rabindra-Jibani o Rabindra-Sahitya Prabeshak*, vols. 1&2, 3rd edition, Calcutta:Visva-Bharati, 1991.

Niederland, W., 'Psychoanalytic approaches to artistic creativity,' *Psychoanal. Q.*, 45, 1976, 193-95.

Nietzsche, F.W., *Daybreak*, tr. R.J. Hollingdale, Cambridge: Cambridge U. Press, 1982.

—— *Beyond Good and Evil*, NP: New Vision, 2007.

Oatley, K. & A. Kerr, 'Memories Prompted by Emotions— Emotions attached to Memories', *Journal of American Academy of Psychoanalysis and Dynamic Psychiatry*, 27(4), 1999, 657-69.

Oremland, J., *The Origins and Psychodynamics of Creativity: A Psychoanalytic Perspective*, Madison, CT.: Int. U. Press, 1997.

Parkinson, T., 'Loneliness of the Poet', in eds., J. Hartog, J.R. Audy and Y.A. Cohen, *The Anatomy of Loneliness*, New York: Int. University Press, 1980.

Pal, P. K., *Rabijibani*, vols.1, 2 and 3, Kolkata: Ananda Publishers, 2006.

Ramachandran, V.S., and W. Hirstein, 'The science of art: A neurological theory of aesthetic experience', *Journal of Consciousness Studies*, 6 (6–7), 1999, 15–51.

—— and E.M. Hubbard, 'Synaesthesia: A window into perception, thought and language', *Journal of Consciousness Studies*, 8 (12), 2001, 3–34.

Rose, G., *Necessary Illusion: Art as Witness*, Madison, CT: IUP, 1996.

Rothenburg, A., *The Emerging Goddess: The Creative Process in Art, Science, and Other Fields*, Chicago: University of Chicago Press,1979.

Roy, K., 'Rabindranath Tagore's emergence as an artist', in *Rabindranath Thakur*, New Delhi: National Gallery of Modern Art, 1981.

Shahly, V., 'Pregnant with Joy and Sorrow: Creativity, Androgyny, and Manic-Depression,' *Annual of Psychoanalysis*, 1988, 16, 289-318.

Scheff, T.J., *Catharsis in Healing, Ritual and Drama*, Berkeley, CA.: University of California Press,1979.

Stoller, R.J., *Perversion*, New York: Pantheon, 1975.

Strachey, L., 'Macaulay', in *Portraits in Miniature: and Other Essays*, London: Chatto and Windus, 1931.

Tagore, D., *The Autobiography of Maharshi Devendranath Tagore*, tr. S.N. Tagore and Indira Devi, London: Macmillan, 1916.

Tagore, R.

—— *Sadhana: the realization of life*, London: Macmillan, 1913.

—— *Fruit-Gathering*, London: Macmillan, 1916.

—— *Stray Birds*, New York: Macmillan, 1916.

—— *Balaka (Wild Geese)*, 1916

—— *My Reminiscences*, tr. S. N. Tagore, New York: Macmillan, 1917.

—— *The Fugitive*, New York: Macmillan, 1921.

—— *Creative Unity*, London: Macmillan, 1922.

—— *The Crescent Moon*, London: Macmillan, 1924.

—— 'The Postmaster', in *The Postmaster: Selected Stories*, tr. W. Radice, Delhi: Penguin, 1991.

—— *Selected Poems*, tr. W. Radice, Delhi: Penguin Books, 1994.

—— *The English Writings of Rabindranath Tagore*, ed. S. K. Das, New Delhi: Sahitya Akadem1, vol. 3, 1996.

—— *The Home and the World*, tr. S. Tagore, New Delhi: Penguin, 1999.

—— *Selected Poems*, ed. S. Choudhuri, New Delhi: Oxford University Press, 2004.

—— *Of Myself* (Atamaparichay), tr. D. Joardar and J. Winter, Shantiniketan: Visva-Bharati, 2006.

—— *Boyhood Days*, tr. R. Chakravarty, Delhi: Puffin, 2007.

—— *Letters from a Sojourner in Europe*, tr. M. Chakravarty, Shantiniketan: Visva-Bharati, 2008.

—— *Three Novellas*, tr. S. Ray, New Delhi : Oxford University Press, 2010.

—— *Gitanjali*, tr. W. Radice, New Delhi: Penguin, 2011.

—— *Selected Plays*, 2 vols., e-book, Centaur, 2011.

—— *Rabindra Chitravali: The Paintings of Rabindranath Tagore*, 4 vols., ed. R. Shiva Kumar, Kolkata: Pratikshan, 2012.

—— *Chithi Patra*, vol.5, Calcutta: Visva-Bharati Grantham Vibhag.

Vygotsky, L.S., *The Psychology of Art*, Cambridge, MA.: MIT Press, 1971.

Wilde, O., 'Preface' to *The Picture of Dorian Gray*, New York: Pocket Books, 2005

Winer, J. A., and J.W. Anderson, eds. 'Psychoanalysis and History', *Annual of Psychoanalysis*, XXXI, Hillsdale, N.J.: Analytic Press, 2003.

Winnicott, D.W., 'The Capacity to be Alone', *Int. J. Psychoanal.*, 39, 1958, 416-20.

Index